S0-BAL-514

English in Action

1

Barbara H. Foley

Elizabeth R. Neblett

HEINLE
CENGAGE Learning

Australia • Brazil • Japan • Korea • Mexico • Singapore • Spain • United Kingdom • United States

English in Action 1
by Barbara H. Foley and Elizabeth R. Neblett

Publisher: Sherrise Roehr

Acquisitions Editor: Tom Jefferies

Assistant Editor: Marissa Petrarca

Director of Content and Media Production: Michael Burggren

Executive Marketing Manager, U.S: Jim McDonough

Product Marketing Manager: Katie Kelley

Sr. Content Project Manager: Maryellen E. Killeen

Sr. Print Buyer: Susan Spencer

Cover / Text Designer: Muse Group, Inc.

Compositor: Pre-PressPMG

© 2010 Cengage Learning

ALL RIGHTS RESERVED. No part of this work covered by the copyright herein may be reproduced, transmitted, stored or used in any form or by any means graphic, electronic, or mechanical, including but not limited to photocopying, recording, scanning, digitizing, taping, Web distribution, information networks, or information storage and retrieval system, except as permitted under Section 107 or 108 of the 1976 United States Copyright Act, without the prior written permission of the publisher.

For product information and technology assistance, contact us at
Cengage Learning Customer & Sales Support, 1-800-354-9706
For permission to use material from this text or product, submit all requests online at **cengage.com/permissions**
Further permissions requests can be emailed to
permissionrequest@cengage.com

Library of Congress Control Number: 2009937466

ISBN-13: 978-1-4240-4990-5
ISBN-10: 1-4240-4990-3

Cengage Learning
20 Channel Center Street
Boston, MA 02210

Cengage Learning is a leading provider of customized learning solutions with office locations around the globe, including Singapore, the United Kingdom, Australia, Mexico, Brazil, and Japan. Locate your office at:
international.cengage.com/region

Cengage Learning products are represented in Canada by Nelson Education, Ltd.

Visit Heinle online at **elt.heinle.com**
Visit our corporate website at **cengage.com**

Printed in the United States
1 2 3 4 5 6 7 13 12 11 10 09

Acknowledgments

The authors and publisher would like to thank the following reviewers and consultants:

Karin Abell
*Durham Technical Community College,
Durham, NC*

Sandra Anderson
El Monte-Rosemead Adult School, El Monte, CA

Sandra Andreessen
Merced Adult School, Merced, CA

Julie Barrett
Madison Area Technical College, Madison, WI

Bea Berretini
Fresno Adult School, Fresno, CA

Mark Brik
*College of Mount Saint Vincent, The Institute for
Immigrant Concerns, New York, NY*

Debra Brooks
BEGIN Managed Programs, Brooklyn, NY

Rocio Castiblanco
*Seminole Community College / Orange County
Public Schools, Sanford, FL*

Sandy Cropper
Fresno Adult School, Fresno, CA

Carol Culver
*Central New Mexico Community College,
Albuquerque, NM*

Luciana Diniz
Portland Community College, Portland, OR

Gail Ellsworth
Milwaukee Area Technical College, Oak Creek, WI

Sally Gearhart
Santa Rosa Junior College, Santa Rosa, CA

Jeane Hetland
Merced Adult School, Merced, CA

Laura Horani
Portland Community College, Portland, OR

Bill Hrycyna
*Franklin Community Adult School,
Los Angeles, CA*

Callie Hutchinson
Sunrise Tech Center, Citrus Heights, CA

Mary Jenison
Merced Adult School, Merced, CA

Mark Labinski
Fox Valley Technical College, Appleton, WI

Rhonda Labor
Northside Learning Center, San Antonio, TX

Lisa Lor
Merced Adult School, Merced, CA

Eileen McKee
Westchester Community College, Valhalla, NY

Jennifer Newman-Cornell
College of Southern Nevada, Las Vegas, NV

Sonja Pantry
Robert Morgan Educational Center, Miami, FL

Eric Rosenbaum
BEGIN Managed Programs, Brooklyn, NY

Jodi Ruback
College of Southern Nevada, Las Vegas, NV

Linda Salem
Northside Learning Center, San Antonio, TX

Evelyn Trottier
*Seattle Central Community College,
Lynnwood, WA*

Maliheh Vafai
Overfelt Adult Center, San Jose, CA

Nancy Williams
Bakersfield Adult School, Bakersfield, CA

Contents

Contents

To the Teacher

English in Action 2nd edition is a four-level core language series for English language learners. It is a comprehensive revision and expansion of *English in Action 1st edition*. The revision has allowed us, the authors, an opportunity to refine the text. We are writers, but we are also teachers. When writing a unit, we can immediately try it out in the classroom. Activities, tasks, and exercises are added, deleted, and changed in an on-going process. Students provide daily and honest feedback.

This first book is designed for students who have had little exposure to English, including new arrivals or adults who have lived in the United States for many years, but have never formally studied English. The text assumes that students are literate in their native language.

The units in Book 1 branch from self, to school, family, home, jobs, and community. The contexts are everyday places and situations. The units build gradually, giving students the vocabulary, the grammar, and the expressions to talk about the situations and themselves. Students see, hear, and practice the language of everyday life in a great variety of exercises and activities. Because this is the first book and students are unsure of themselves, there is ever-present support in the form of grammar notes, examples, vocabulary boxes, and so on. By the end of Book 1, students should feel comfortable talking, reading, and writing about their lives using basic English phrases and sentences.

Each unit will take between five and seven hours of classroom time. If you have less time, you may need to choose the exercises you feel are the most appropriate for your students. You can assign some of the activities for homework. For example, after previewing **Writing Our Stories**, students can write their own stories at home, instead of in class. The short descriptions that follow give you an idea of the sections in each unit.

Finally, the book comes with an audio component. The listening activities in the units are motivating and interesting. They provide other voices than that of the teacher. We have encouraged our adult students to buy the book / audio package. They tell us that they listen to the audio at home and in the car.

Changes to this Edition

There are three new or adapted units in the second edition. Unit 9: Transportation is a brand new unit. The students discuss different modes of transporta-tion, and how they get to and from class, home, and work. The grammar focus is on present continuous questions. In Unit 11, students talk about their daily schedules and study routines. Students talk about when, where, and how to study. The grammar focus is simple present tense. Several teachers requested that the future tense be included in Book 1, and Unit 15 is a new unit that fulfills this need. In Unit 15, students talk about their weekend plans and activi-ties in their communities. The grammar focus is the future tense with *be going to*.

The new features in the second edition include:

- **Word Builder** is an opportunity for students to practice the Dictionary vocabulary.
- **Word Partnerships** are word collocations related to the Dictionary vocabulary.
- **Working Together** activities are partner and group activities that are now spread throughout the units. Look for the partner icons.
- **Sharing Our Stories** allows students to read and talk about each other's writing.
- **English in Action** is a two-page spread that gives students practice in life skills related to the topic of the unit. For example, in Clothing and Weather, students practice returning items to a clothing store. In A Visit to the Doctor, they make a doc-tor's appointment and fill out a patient informa-tion form.

Dictionary

Each unit opens with a one- or two-page illustrated **Dictionary**. Students are asked to listen and repeat each item. Teachers realize that one repetition of vocabulary words does not produce mastery. Ask stu-dents to sit in groups and study the words together. Stage spelling bees. Play word bingo. Look for the same items in the classroom or school environment. Students must also study the words at home.

Word Partnerships

This is a new feature, which usually appears at the end of the **Dictionary** section. It provides students with common high-frequency collocations using vocabulary from the **Dictionary**. Have students practice using these collocations in sentences of their own creation.

Word Builder

This is another new feature that provides additional practice with the vocabulary from the **Dictionary**.

Have students refer to the **Dictionary** if they need help completing these activities. Many of the activities in this section include structures from the unit and recycle the grammar from previous units.

Active Grammar

Three to six pages of structured exercises and activities present and practice the grammar of the unit. This first book integrates the new vocabulary and the grammar throughout all the activities in the unit. At this level, grammar mastery is not the goal, but rather an introduction to the basic structures of English and a feeling of comfort and security in the new language. As students progress through this section, they will find a variety of supportive features. Artwork and photos illustrate the context clearly. Word boxes show the verbs or nouns to use in the answers. Those who have used the first edition will see that there is enhanced grammar support within the units with full, colored grammar charts and sample sentences. In addition, students can look at the grammar charts in the appendix for a summary of all the grammatical points covered in the book.

For many of the exercises, the entire class will be working together with your direction and explanations. Other exercises have a partner icon—students can try these with another student.

Working Together

Working Together activities are more cooperative, encouraging students to work in groups, role play, or exchange information in a more active way. You can walk around the classroom, listening to students and answering their questions. Encourage this free flow of the language, replete with mistakes and hesitancies, as it is an important step in gaining comfort and fluency in English. If your students represent several different languages, group students with classmates who speak a language other than their own.

Pronunciation

Within the **Active Grammar** section is an exercise that focuses on pronunciation. These are specific pronunciation points that complement the grammar or vocabulary of the lesson, such as the sound of plural *s*, contractions, numbers, syllables, and so on.

The Big Picture

This is our favorite section. It integrates listening, vocabulary, and structure. A large, engaging picture shows a particular setting, such as a restaurant, a doctor's office, or an office supply store. Students listen to a short story or conversation, and then answer questions about the story, fill in exercises, review structures, or write conversations.

Reading

A short reading expands the context of the lesson. We did not manipulate a selection so that every sentence fits into the structure presented in the unit! There are new vocabulary words and structures. Teachers can help readers learn that understanding the main idea is primary. They can then go back over the material to find the details that are interesting or relevant. If students can find the information they need, it is not necessary to master or look up every word.

Writing Our Stories

In this writing section, students first read a paragraph written by an English language learner or teacher. By using checklists or fill-in sentences, students are directed to brainstorm about their own schools, families, jobs, and so on. Students then have an opportunity to write about themselves. Several teachers have told us about the creative ways they share student writing, including publishing student magazines, designing a class Web page, and displaying stories and photos taken by their students. *Sharing Our Stories* directs students to read and understand one another's stories.

English in Action

The unit concludes with a two-page **English in Action** section. It provides practice in the everyday skills students need to interact as citizens, family members, students, and workers. The activities that follow include role plays, forms, and problem-solving exercises to help students become more comfortable in these real-life situations.

The complete *English in Action* package includes everything necessary for students and teachers to facilitate learning. Visit elt.heinle.com to learn more about available resources.

Fun, engaging, and action-packed!

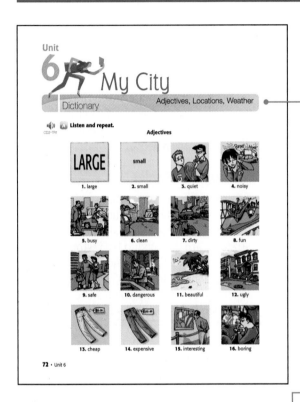

A **"Dictionary"** section begins each chapter with a picture dictionary–style presentation of key vocabulary words to illuminate word meaning.

NEW TO THIS EDITION!

"Word Partnerships" provide students with frequent collocations to promote fluency.

NEW TO THIS EDITION!

"Word Builder" activities provide additional vocabulary practice and encourage students to get a deeper understanding of the target words.

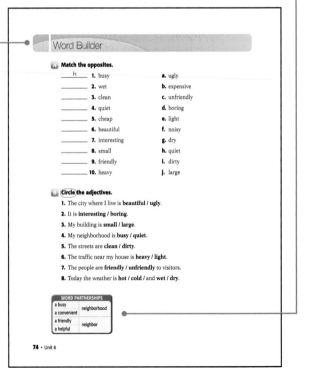

Fun, engaging, and action-packed!

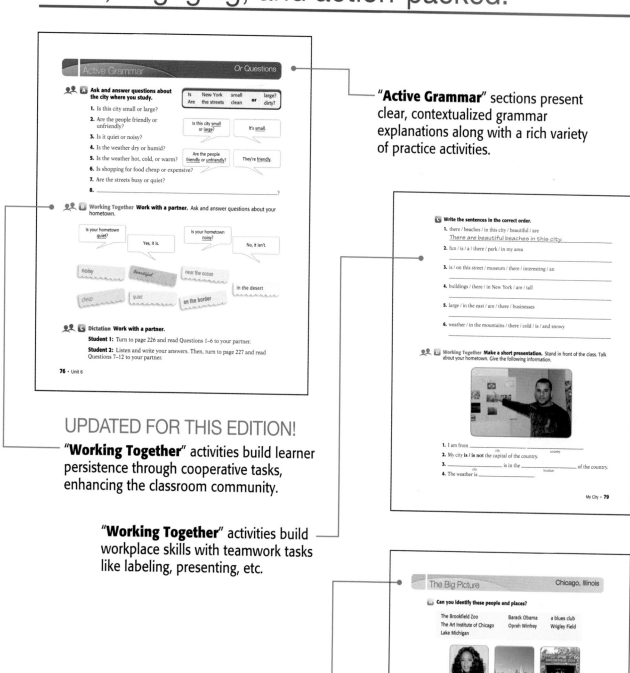

"Active Grammar" sections present clear, contextualized grammar explanations along with a rich variety of practice activities.

UPDATED FOR THIS EDITION!

"Working Together" activities build learner persistence through cooperative tasks, enhancing the classroom community.

"Working Together" activities build workplace skills with teamwork tasks like labeling, presenting, etc.

"The Big Picture" sections include integrated skills practice around a story or conversation, motivating students to listen and use new grammar and vocabulary.

Fun, engaging, and action-packed!

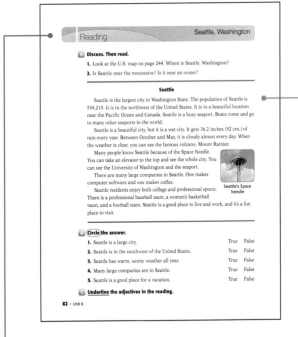

Interesting readings based on the unit theme recycle the vocabulary and grammar presented earlier in the unit.

"Reading" sections provide before-you-read discussion questions encouraging students to think about the reading topic.

"Writing Our Stories" sections expand students' literacy by giving a closer look at real people in real communities and guided, practice activities to help students write about themselves.

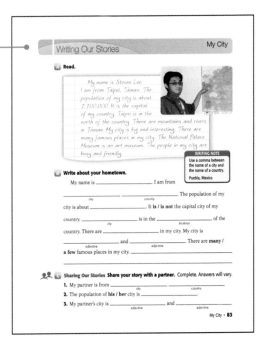

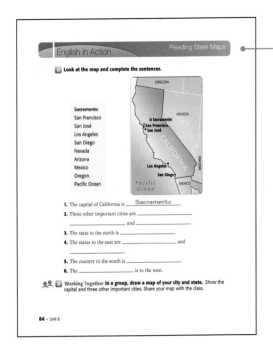

NEW TO THIS EDITION!
"English in Action" sections practice the everyday skills students need to interact and solve problems in the real world.

About the Authors

Liz and I work at Union County College in Elizabeth, New Jersey. We teach at the Institute for Intensive English, a large English as a Second Language program. Students from over 80 different countries study in our classes. Between us, Liz and I have been teaching at the college for over 40 years! When Liz isn't writing, she spends her time traveling, taking pictures, and worrying about her favorite baseball team, the New York Mets. I love the outdoors. I can't start my day without a 15- or 20-mile bicycle ride. My idea of a good time always involves being active: hiking, swimming, or simply working in my garden. I also enjoy watching my favorite baseball team, the New York Yankees.

Barbara H. Foley
Elizabeth R. Neblett

Photo Credits

pp. xiii, 1–3, 13, 28, 79 Photos courtesy of Elizabeth R. Neblett. All other credits listed top to bottom, left to right. **Unit 1:** p. 9 Eyedear | Dreamstime.com, digitalskillet/istockphoto.com, d9tech/istockphoto.com, michaeljung, 2008/Used under license from Shutterstock.com, Yannp/Dreamstime, Jenkedco/Dreamstime; p. 10 Andresr, 2008/Used under license from Shutterstock.com, d9tech/istockphoto.com; p. 15 Scott Meyer/Alamy, wmiami,2009/Used under license from Shutterstock.com. **Unit 2:** p. 27 Futuredigi... | Dreamstime.com. **Unit 3:** p. 33 VikramRaghuvanshi/istockphoto.com, Roger Lecuyer/istockphoto.com; p. 34 Monkey Business Images, 2009/Used under license from shutterstock.com, manley620/istockphoto.com, digitalskillet/istockphoto.com, Ilona75/Dreamstime LLC; p. 35 darren baker/ istockphoto.com, Kevin Russ/istockphoto.com; p. 37 Spiderstock/istockphoto.com, Rui Vale de Sousa, 2009/Used under license from Shutterstock.com; p. 40 Feverpitch/Dreamstime.com, Ryuhei Shindo/Photonica/Getty Images, Bill Bachmann/Alamy; p. 41 iofoto/ istockphoto.com. **Unit 4:** p. 55 Monkey Business Images,2009/ Used under license from Shutterstock.com, istockphoto.com. **Unit 5:** p. 68 Phil Date/istockphoto.com. **Unit 6:** p. 77 absolut, 2009/Used under license from shutterstock.com, Ricardo A. Alves, 2009/Used under license from shutterstock.com, Cristian Lazzari/istockphoto.com, emin kuliyev, 2009/Used under license from shutterstock.com; p. 80 Astrid Stawiarz/Getty Images, Marc Schlossman/Photographer's Choice/Getty Images, Chuck Eckert/Alamy, Rick Diamond/Getty Images, Dennis Hallinan/Hulton Archive/Getty Images, Kim Karpeles/Alamy, ROBYN BECK/AFP/Getty Images; p. 82 Comstock Images/Jupiter Images. **Unit 7:** p. 96 Bill Aron/PhotoEdit. **Unit 8:** p. 100 and 101 Peter Spiro/istockphoto.com, jackhollingsworthcom, LLC,2009/Used under license from Shutterstock.Com, Loren Lewis,2009/ Used under license from Shutterstock.Com, jackhollingsworthcom, LLC,2009/Used under license from Shutterstock.Com; p. 100 only Christophe Testi,2009/Used under license from Shutterstock.Com, Aaron Amat,2009/Used under license from Shutterstock.Com, sevenke,2009/ Used under license from Shutterstock.Com, Amy Johansson, 2009/Used under license from Shutterstock.com; p. 106 Bobby Deal/RealDeal-Photo, 2008/ Used under license from Shutterstock.com, GWImages, 2009/ Used under license from Shutterstock.com; p. 107 BWAC Images/ Alamy; p. 110 VikramRaghuvanshi/Istockphoto.com, Juanmonino/ istockphoto.com; p. 111 photos.com. **Unit 9:** p. 117 Theodore Anderson/ The Image Bank/Getty Images, Photos.com; p. 124 Don Mason/Blend Images/Jupiter Images; p. 125 Ivan Hunter/Rubberball Productions/ Getty Images. **Unit 10:** p. 130 Catherine Karnow/ CORBIS; p. 134 Jose Luis Pelaez, Inc./Blend Images/Corbis, PhotosIndia.com LLC/Alamy; p. 137 Michael Newman/PhotoEdit; p. 140 Leonid Nyshko/iStockphoto.com, Alexander Kalina/iStockphoto.com, Skip O'Donnell/iStockphoto.com; p. 141 Sean Locke/ istockphoto.com. **Unit 11:** p. 150 Kaz Chiba/Photographer's Choice/Getty Images, Bruce Laurance/Riser/Getty Images, p. 154 michaeljung, 2009/Used under license from Shutterstock.com, Ariel Skelley/Getty Images; p. 155, Monkey Business Images, 2009/Used under license from Shutterstock.com. **Unit 12:** p. 160 Image Source/Jupiter Images; p. 161 Todd Taulman/istockphoto.com, Hall/ photocuisine/Corbis, Terraxplorer/istockphoto.com, Thomas Peterson/Alamy; p. 168 LISA DEJONG/The Plain Dealer/Landov; p. 169 Ariel Skelley/Photographer's Choice/Getty Images. **Unit 13:** p. 176 Derrick A. Bruce/Surf/CORBIS; p. 177 (all 3 photos by) Photos.com; p. 178 Jupiterimages, Amy Eckert/The Image Bank/Getty Images, i love images/Alamy, Simon Jarratt/Ivy/Corbis; p. 181 Photos.com, David Young-Wolff/Stone/Getty Images, John Lund/Blend Images/Jupiter Images, Noel Hendrickson/Jupiter Images; p. 184 Robert Brenner/ PhotoEdit, Diego.cervo/Dreamstime; p. 185 Thinkstock Images/Jupiter Images. **Unit 14:** p. 198 Dmitriy Shironosov, 2009/Used under license from Shutterstock.com; p. 199 Jeremy Woodhouse/Blend Images/Jupiter Images. **Unit 15:** p. 209 AP Photo/Richard Drew, Andrew H. Walker/Getty Images Entertainment /Getty Images, AP Photo/Buda Mendes/Agencia AGIF, Joe Murphy/NBAE via Getty Images, Filippov Alexei/UPPA/ Photoshot, AP Photo/Richard Drew, AP Photo/Tom Gannam, FRANCOIS GUILLOT/AFP/Getty Images; p. 212 Patrick Batchelder/Alamy; p. 213 JGI/Blend Images/Alamy

  A **Listen and repeat.**

CD1•TR1

one student

two students

three students

four students

five students

six students

seven students

eight students

nine students

ten students

A Listen.

CD1•TR2

 B Working Together Introduce yourself to two classmates.

> **A:** Hello. My name is Miguel.
>
> **B:** Hi. I'm Elena.
>
> **A:** Nice to meet you, Elena.
>
> **B:** Nice to meet you, too.

I am = I'm

C Complete.

1. My first name is _____.

2. My last name is _____.

WORD PARTNERSHIPS	
first	
middle	name
last	

Elena Blanco
First Name: Elena
Last Name: Blanco

Word Builder

 A **Listen.** Then, listen again and repeat.

CD1•TR3

Aa	Bb	Cc	Dd	Ee	Ff	Gg
Hh	Ii	Jj	Kk	Ll	Mm	Nn
Oo	Pp	Qq	Rr	Ss	Tt	Uu
Vv	Ww	Xx	Yy	Zz		

A = capital letter

a = lowercase letter

 B **Listen and write the letter you hear.**

CD1•TR4

1. ___C___   4. _____   7. _____

2. _____   5. _____   8. _____

3. _____   6. _____   9. _____

 C **Working Together** **Practice your spelling.**

Student 1 Close your book. Listen to your partner spell names 1–7. Write the names on a sheet of paper. Then spell names 8–15 slowly for your partner.

Student 2 Spell names 1–7 slowly. Now close your book. Listen to your partner spell names 8–15.

1. Paula	**6.** Daniel	**11.** Garcia
2. Carlos	**7.** Joanne	**12.** Walker
3. Victoria	**8.** Anthony	**13.** Mitchell
4. Jeffrey	**9.** Elizabeth	**14.** Brooks
5. Debbie	**10.** William	**15.** Johnson

CD1·TR5

A **Listen and read.**

A: What's your first name?

B: Ana

A: What's your last name?

B: Santos

A: Please spell that.

B: S-A-N-T-O-S

B **Working Together** **Ask five students their names.**
Listen and write their first and last names.

> What's **your** first name?
> What's **your** last name?
> Please spell that.

1. _____   _____

2. _____   _____

3. _____   _____

4. _____   _____

5. _____   _____

C **Read.**

My name is Sandra.   **His** name is Tuan.   **Her** name is Erica.   **Their** names are Serena and James.

D **Say your classmates' names.**

> His name is Tuan.

> Her name is Erica.

> Their names are Serena and James.

Active Grammar

A Read the chart and look at the pictures.

I	**am**	from the United States.
You	**are**	from China.
She	**is**	from Mexico.
They	**are**	from Haiti.

Use *the* with these countries:

the Dominican Republic
the Philippines
the Republic of Congo
the United States
the United Arab Emirates

B Complete with *am / is / are*.

1. They ____are____ from New York.

2. Denise _____ from Greece.

3. Pedro _____ from the Dominican Republic.

4. They _____ from the United States.

5. I _____ from Bogotá, Colombia.

6. My sister and I _____ from Lisbon, Portugal.

7. Mr. Martinez _____ from Boston, Massachusetts.

8. Mr. and Mrs. Martinez _____ from Boston.

9. Miss Lee _____ from Korea.

Mr. Frank Martinez   **Mrs.** Ana Martinez   **Miss** Lily Lee / **Ms.** Lily Lee

C Working Together Work in a large group. Look at the world map on page 245. Ask and answer questions about your countries. Point to your country on the map.

Where are you from?

I'm from the United States.

Where is he from?

He is from Brazil.

D Write about the students in Exercise C.

1. _____Carlos_____ is from _____Columbia_____.

2. _____ is from _____.

3. _____ is from _____.

4. _____ is from _____.

5. _____.

A **Listen and repeat.**

CD1·TR6

I am	⟶	I'm
you are	⟶	you're
he is	⟶	he's
she is	⟶	she's
it is	⟶	it's
we are	⟶	we're
they are	⟶	they're

  B **Pronunciation: Contractions** **Listen and repeat.**

CD1·TR7

1. He is from Mexico. ⟶ He's from Mexico.

2. She is from Vietnam. ⟶ She's from Vietnam.

3. I am from Russia. ⟶ I'm from Russia.

4. He is from China. ⟶ He's from China.

5. I am from Haiti. ⟶ I'm from Haiti.

6. She is from Peru. ⟶ She's from Peru.

7. He is from Cuba. ⟶ He's from Cuba.

8. She is from Egypt. ⟶ She's from Egypt.

  C **Dictation** **Listen and complete.**

CD1·TR8

1. ___I am___ from Mexico. **5.** _____ from Ukraine.

2. _____ from Alaska. **6.** _____ from Italy.

3. _____ from Chile. **7.** _____ from Vietnam.

4. _____ from Cameroon. **8.** _____ from Colombia.

A **Ask and answer the questions with a partner.**

Min (China)

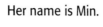
Her name is Min.

She's from China.

1. What's her name?
Where is she from?

Adolfo and
Alfredo
(El Salvador)

2. What are their names?
Where are they from?

Hong (Vietnam)

3. What's his name?
Where is he from?

Aruna (India)

4. What's her name?
Where is she from?

John (Canada)

5. What's his name?
Where is he from?

Rosa and
Consuelo
(Guatemala)

6. What are their names?
Where are they from?

Mirror

7. What's your name?
Where are you from?

The USA

A Write.

a. His first name is Hong.

b. ~~Her first name is Luisa.~~

c. Her last name is Reyes.

d. His last name is Lin.

e. His street address is 12 Bay Street.

f. Her ID number is 44387.

g. She is a student at Edison School.

h. He lives in Tampa, Florida.

i. His zip code is 33615.

1. Her first name is Luisa.

2. _____

3. _____

4. _____

1. _____

2. _____

3. _____

4. _____

5. _____

B Match.

___c___ **1.** What's his name?

_____ **2.** Where is he from?

_____ **3.** What's her name?

_____ **4.** Where is she from?

_____ **5.** What's your name?

_____ **6.** Where are you from?

a. Her name is Imelda.

b. He is from Mexico.

c. His name is Hector.

d. I'm from Poland.

e. She is from the Philippines.

f. My name is Dorota.

A **Listen.**
CD1·TR9

_____ _____ _____ _____ _____

B **Listen again and write each person's name.**
CD1·TR9

| Tomás | Hiro | Erica | Marie | Jenny |

C **Listen and write the answers.**
CD1·TR10

1. _____Tomás_____   **3.** _____   **5.** _____

2. _____   **4.** _____   **6.** _____

D **Listen.** Write the number next to the correct answer.
CD1·TR11

_____ **a.** He is from Japan.

_____ **b.** I'm from Peru.

_____ **c.** His name is Hiro.

_____ **d.** Her name is Marie.

___1___ **e.** My name is Tomás.

_____ **f.** She's from Haiti.

Reading

A (Circle) **the countries where English is spoken.**

(the United States)   Japan   China   Mexico

Colombia   Britain   Ireland   India

Australia   Russia   Canada   South Africa

B **Read.**

English Around the World

Many people around the world speak English as their first language. People in the United States, Great Britain, Ireland, and Australia speak English.

In India, there are 21 official languages, but English is the language of politics and business. In South Africa, there are many languages, too, but many people speak English.

For you, English is a new language, but you can speak some English, too. You know words like *car, man, woman,* and *money.* You know sentences such as, *I'm a student* and *I'm from Mexico.*

English is a language with different words and new grammar. It will take time to learn. Many people around the world speak English. Soon you will speak English, too.

C **Complete the sentences.**

English   grammar   languages   ~~People~~   world

1. _____People_____ in the United States and Australia speak English.

2. In India, there are 21 official _____.

3. Many people around the _____ speak English.

4. English has new _____.

5. Soon you will speak _____ too.

Writing Our Stories

 Read.

My name is Antonio. I am from
Mexico. I am studying English.
I am a student at Bayside Adult
School. My teacher is Ms. Johnson.

B Write.

My name is _____ _____.
                first name   last name

I am from _____. I am studying English. I am a student at
           country

_____. My teacher's name is _____.
    name of school   name

Margins

Full Name
Date

Title

WRITING NOTE
Use margins when you write.

C Sharing Our Stories Read your partner's story. Complete the information below.

1. Her / His name is _____ _____.

2. She / He is from _____.

English in Action

 A **Listen and repeat.**

CD1·TR12

0	1	2	3	4	5	6	7	8	9	10
zero	one	two	three	four	five	six	seven	eight	nine	ten

11	12	13	14	15	16	17	18	19	20
eleven	twelve	thirteen	fourteen	fifteen	sixteen	seventeen	eighteen	nineteen	twenty

  B **Listen and write the numbers.**

CD1·TR13

a. _____6_____   i. _____

b. _____   j. _____

c. _____   k. _____

d. _____   l. _____

e. _____   m. _____

f. _____   n. _____

g. _____   o. _____

h. _____

C **Listen and write the words for the numbers.**

CD1·TR14

a. ____ten____   f. _____

b. _____   g. _____

c. _____   h. _____

d. _____   i. _____

e. _____

A **Listen and read.**

CD1·TR15

CULTURE NOTE

In a telephone number, say each number separately.

What's your telephone number?

My telephone number is 301-555-1796.

301-555-1796?

Yes, that's right.

Thank you.

 B **Listen and write.**

CD1·TR16

a. 5 5 5 - 3 2 3 1

b. _ _ _ - _ _ _ _

c. _ _ _ - _ _ _ - _ _ _ _

d. _ _ _ - _ _ _ - _ _ _ _

e. _ _ _ - _ _ _ _

f. _ _ _ - _ _ _ _

g. _ _ _ - _ _ _ - _ _ _ _

h. _ _ _ - _ _ _ - _ _ _ _

C **Complete.**

A B C

Name _____

Phone _____

Fax _____

Email _____

Address _____

_____

The Classroom

Dictionary

Classroom Objects

🔊 **A** **Listen and repeat.**

CD1·TR17

20. a clock

17. a pencil sharpener

15. a map

1. a wall

19. a window

2. a board

4. a piece of chalk

3. an eraser

5. a teacher

18. a door

14. a bookcase

6. a desk

8. a printer

16. an umbrella

9. a student

10. a table

13. a chair

7. a computer

11. a cell phone

12. a backpack

CD1·TR18

B **Listen and repeat.**

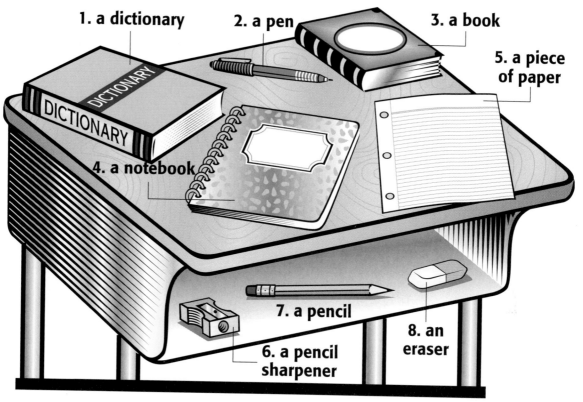

1. a dictionary
2. a pen
3. a book
4. a notebook
5. a piece of paper
6. a pencil sharpener
7. a pencil
8. an eraser

C **Circle the items that are in your classroom.**
Add to the list.

1. a table
2. a chair
3. a world map
4. a U.S. map
5. a clock
6. a computer
7. a pencil sharpener
8. a chalkboard

9. a white board
10. a dictionary
11. a window
12. a bookcase
13. _____
14. _____
15. _____
16. _____

WORD PARTNERSHIPS	
erase	a mistake the board
sharpen	a pencil
open	a book
close	a dictionary

Word Builder

A Write.

1.
 a book

2.

3.

4.

5.

6.

7.

8.

9.

10.

CD1·TR19

B Listen and complete.

pen   notebook

piece of paper   pencil sharpener

~~dictionary~~

1. Is this your ___dictionary___?
   Yes, it is. Thank you.

2. Is this your _____?
   Yes, it is. Thank you.

3. Is this your _____?
   No, it isn't.

4. Is this your _____?
   Yes, _____ _____. Thank you.

5. Is this your _____?
   No, _____ _____.

C Working Together **Work with a group.** Find items in your backpack or purse. Put them on the desk. Ask and answer questions.

Is this your cell phone?

Yes, it is. Thank you.

Is this your pen?

No, it isn't.

Article	Singular Noun
a	book
	student
an	eraser
	umbrella

Use *a* before a noun that begins with a consonant sound.

Use *an* before a noun that begins with a vowel sound: a, e, i, o, u.

Do not use *a* or *an* with plural nouns.

 A **Listen and repeat.**

CD1·TR20

1.

a book   books

4.

a man   men

2.

a pencil   pencils

5.

a woman   women

3.

a student   students

6.

a child   children

B **Write *a* or *an*.** Write *X* if no article is necessary.

1. ____*a*____ teacher

2. _____ book

3. _____ pencil sharpener

4. _____ Florida

5. _____ umbrella

6. _____ Mr. Gonzalez

7. _____ computers

8. _____ student

9. _____ erasers

10. _____ backpacks

Do not use *a* or *the* with most proper nouns.

California
Tom
Mrs. Smith

Active Grammar

Plural Nouns
books
students
erasers
umbrellas

Irregular Plural Forms

child	children
man	men
woman	women

Add *s* to the end of a noun to make it plural. Some plural nouns have an irregular form.

CD1·TR21

A **Pronunciation: Plural Nouns** **Listen and circle.**

1. (a pencil)   pencils
2. a student   students
3. a teacher   teachers
4. a man   men
5. a map   maps

6. a dictionary   dictionaries
7. an eraser   erasers
8. a notebook   notebooks
9. a classroom   classrooms
10. a woman   women

B **Say the words in Exercise A.**

C **Circle.**

1.

a table   tables

3.

an eraser   erasers

5.

a pencil   pencils

2.

a clock   clocks

4.

a woman   women

6.

a book   books

D **Write the plural forms.**

1. child ___children___
2. man _____
3. desk _____
4. student _____

5. dictionary _____
6. umbrella _____
7. woman _____
8. clock _____

E Write.

1. _pencils_

2. _____

3. _____

4. _____

5. _____

6. _____

7. _____

8. _____

F Write *a* or *an*. Write *X* if no article is necessary.

1. ___*a*___ chair
2. _____ table
3. _____ desk
4. _____ Mr. James
5. _____ eraser

6. _____ students
7. _____ teacher
8. _____ pen
9. _____ bookcases
10. _____ white board

11. _____ Texas
12. _____ printer
13. _____ cell phone
14. _____ umbrella
15. _____ dictionary

G Working Together **Work with a group.** Look around your classroom. Write plural nouns.

1. _____
2. _____
3. _____

4. _____
5. _____
6. _____

This is my book.

These are your books.

Use *this* with a singular noun.
Use *these* with plural nouns.

A Complete.

1. ___This is___ my chair.

2. ___These are___ your books.

3. _____ your pencils.

4. _____ my backpack.

5. _____ her notebook.

6. _____ his erasers.

7. _____ my dictionary.

8. _____ her dictionaries.

B Ask and answer questions with a partner.

Is this your pencil?

Yes, it is.

Are these your books?

No, they aren't.

1.

2.

3.

4.

5.

6.

There	**is**	a student	in the classroom.
	are	students	

> Use *there is* and *there are* to talk about a room, city, or other place.

 Complete.

1. ___There are___ two students in the classroom.

2. _____ a student from France in the room.

3. _____ twenty desks in my classroom.

4. _____ books in the bookcase.

5. _____ a dictionary on the desk.

6. _____ one pencil sharpener in the room.

7. _____ a woman in the classroom.

8. _____ five men in the class.

 Listen and (circle) Desk 1 or Desk 2.

CD1·TR22

Desk 1

Desk 2

1.	(Desk 1)	Desk 2		5.	Desk 1	Desk 2
2.	Desk 1	Desk 2		6.	Desk 1	Desk 2
3.	Desk 1	Desk 2		7.	Desk 1	Desk 2
4.	Desk 1	Desk 2		8.	Desk 1	Desk 2

 Working Together Work with a group. Write three true sentences and three false sentences about your classroom. Then, read your sentences to the class. Your classmates will say, "True" or "False."

There are 100 students in this class.

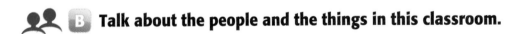

A Circle the things you see in this classroom.

a computer	a woman	a pencil	a window
a board	a clock	a teacher	a man
a table	a book	a U.S. map	children
a pencil sharpener	a door	desks	

B Talk about the people and the things in this classroom.

C Listen and look at the picture.

CD1 · TR23

◀))) **D** **Listen and circle.**

CD1·TR24

1. True (False)   **4.** True   False   **7.** True   False

2. True   False   **5.** True   False   **8.** True   False

3. True   False   **6.** True   False   **9.** True   False

◀))) **E** **Listen.** If the information is correct, write the sentence. If the information is wrong, put an *X*.

CD1·TR25

1. _X_____

2. _____

3. _____

4. _____

5. _____

6. _____

7. _____

8. _____

F **Complete.**

clock	clocks	student	students
map	~~maps~~	man	men
woman	women	desk	desks

1. There are two _____*maps*_____ on the wall.

2. There is a _____ of the world.

3. There are ten _____ in the class.

4. There are four _____ and six _____.

5. There is one _____ from India.

6. There are twelve _____ in the classroom.

7. There is a _____ on the wall.

The Classroom · **25**

A **Read the school signs.** Ask your teacher about any new signs.

 **MEN**

WOMEN

 PULL **FIRE** ALARM

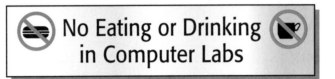 No Eating or Drinking in Computer Labs

Join The Tennis Club
See Dave Coles
Room 341

 **NO SMOKING**

LIBRARY HOURS

Monday to Friday	9:00 A.M. to 10:00 P.M.
Saturday	9:00 A.M. to 5:00 P.M.
Sunday	1:00 P.M. to 5:00 P.M.

 B **Working Together** **Work with a group.** Walk around your school. Copy three signs that you see.

A **Read.**

> I study English at the English Adult School. My class is very large. There are 30 students in my class. We are from 20 different countries. We speak ten different languages.
>
> Our classroom is small. There are 30 small desks. Our teacher, Mrs. Garcia, has a large desk for her books and her papers. We have many pencils, but we don't have a pencil sharpener. We are from many countries, but we don't have a map on the wall.
>
> We need a larger classroom with a pencil sharpener and a map.

WRITING NOTE
Use a period at the end of every sentence.

B **Write about your classroom.**

I study English at _____. There
name of your school

are _____ students in my class. We are from
number

_____ different countries. We speak _____
number   number

different languages.

Our classroom is _____. There are _____
big / small   number

desks in the classroom. There is _____ _____. There
a / an

_____.

 C **Sharing Our Stories** **Read a partner's story.** Check for a period at the end of each sentence.

A **Listen.** Write the number of the classroom direction.

CD1·TR26

a. _____   d. _____   g. _____

b. _____   e. _____   h. _____

c. _____   f. _____   i. _____

B **Write each sentence under the correct picture in Exercise A.**

Erase the board.	Sharpen your pencil.	Close your book.
Use the computer.	Erase your mistake.	Put away your cell phone.
Write on the board.	Open your book.	~~Raise your hand~~.

C **Working Together** **Work with a group.** Take turns acting out classroom directions. Your classmates will guess the correct action.

A **Listen and repeat.**

CD1·TR27

1	2	3	4	5	6	7	8	9	10
one	two	three	four	five	six	seven	eight	nine	ten
11	12	13	14	15	16	17	18	19	20
eleven	twelve	thirteen	fourteen	fifteen	sixteen	seventeen	eighteen	nineteen	twenty
21	22	23	24	25	26	27	28	29	30
twenty-one	twenty-two	twenty-three	twenty-four	twenty-five	twenty-six	twenty-seven	twenty-eight	twenty-nine	thirty

10	20	30	40	50	60	70	80	90	100	1,000
ten	twenty	thirty	forty	fifty	sixty	seventy	eighty	ninety	one hundred	one thousand

B **Say the words.** Then, write the numbers.

1. twenty-six ___26___

2. thirty-three _____

3. forty-nine _____

4. one hundred _____

5. one hundred-ten _____

6. two hundred-fifty _____

7. one thousand four hundred _____

8. one thousand ninety _____

C **Write.**

1. 36 __thirty-six__

2. 51 _____

3. 101 _____

4. 750 _____

5. 300 _____

6. 1000 _____

D **Take turns dictating numbers to a partner.**

1. Write five large numbers. Read them slowly to your partner.

2. Listen and write the numbers. Then, change roles.

Unit 3

The Family

Dictionary

A Family Tree

  A **Listen and repeat.**

CD1·TR28

The Sanchez Family

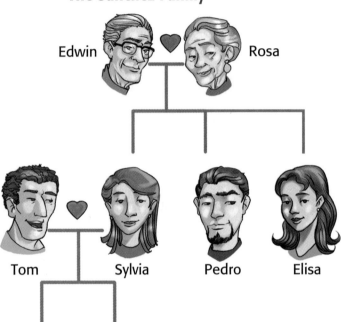

Edwin   Rosa

Tom   Sylvia   Pedro   Elisa

Annie   Eric

The Family

1. husband
2. wife
3. father
4. mother
5. son
6. daughter
7. brother
8. sister
9. grandfather
10. grandmother
11. grandson
12. granddaughter
13. uncle
14. aunt
15. nephew
16. niece

 **B** **Listen and repeat.**

CD1·TR29

1. single   **2.** married   **3.** divorced

mother = mom
father = dad
mother + father = parents

WORD PARTNERSHIPS	
an older	brother
a younger	sister

Word Builder

A **Complete.**

Male	Female
son	_daughter_
uncle	_____
_____	grandmother
brother	_____
_____	wife
_____	granddaughter
nephew	_____
_____	_____

B **Complete.**

1. Eric and Annie are _____ _brother and sister_ _____.

2. Edwin and Rosa are _____.

3. Rosa and Sylvia are _____.

4. Edwin and Pedro are _____.

5. Pedro and Eric are _____.

6. Rosa and Annie are _____.

7. Edwin and Eric are _____.

8. Annie and Elisa are _____.

C **Listen and (circle) the correct name.**

CD1 • TR30

1. a. Tom **b.** Pedro   **4. a.** Sylvia **b.** Annie   **7. a.** Pedro **b.** Edwin

2. a. Rosa **b.** Sylvia   **5. a.** Elisa **b.** Annie   **8. a.** Rosa **b.** Elisa

3. a. Tom **b.** Pedro   **6. a.** Tom **b.** Edwin   **9. a.** Eric **b.** Tom

  D **Working Together** **Draw your family tree.** Tell your partner about your family.

Listen and repeat.

CD1·TR31

1. He's tall.　　**2.** He's short.　　　　**3.** She's heavy.　　**4.** She's thin.

5. He's young.　　　　**6.** He's old.

7. Her hair is long.　　　　**8.** Her hair is short.
　　 She has long hair.　　　　　　 She has short hair.

9. Her hair is straight.　　**10.** Her hair is curly.　　**11.** Her hair is wavy.

12. He has a beard.　　**13.** He has a moustache.　　**14.** He's bald.

A **Complete.**

1. I am _____tall_____. (tall / medium height / short)

2. I am _____. (thin / average weight / heavy)

3. I am _____. (young / middle aged / old)

4. My hair is _____. (blond / brown / black / red / gray)

5. I have _____ hair. (short / long / medium-length)

6. My hair is _____. (straight / wavy / curly)

blond

brown

black

red

gray

B **Circle.**

1. She's **tall / medium height / short**.

2. She's **thin / average weight / heavy**.

3. She is **young / middle aged / old**.

4. Her hair is _____. (color)

5. She has **short / long** hair.

6. Her hair is **straight / wavy / curly**.

C **Circle.**

1. He's **tall / medium height / short**.

2. He's **thin / average weight / heavy**.

3. He is **young / middle aged / old**.

4. His hair is _____. (color)

5. He has **short / long** hair.

6. His hair is **straight / wavy / curly**.

7. He has a _____.

 D **Working Together** **Work with a small group.** Bring in a picture of a famous person from a newspaper or a magazine. Describe the person.

How old	are	you?	I'm	19.
	is	he?	He's	7.

A Read.

Margaret: This is my son, Nico.

Kathy: How old is he?

Margaret: He's 3. And this is my daughter, Alexa.

Kathy: How old is she?

Margaret: She's 7.

Kathy: You have a beautiful family.

CULTURE NOTE

We ask the ages of children and young people. We do not ask the age of an adult.

CD1·TR32

B **Listen.** Number the photographs. Then, listen again and write the relationships and ages.

Relationship	Age
daughter	35

Relationship	Age

Relationship	Age

ID Cards

A **Complete.**

1. Her first name is _____.

2. Her last name is _____.

3. Her hair is _____.

4. Her eyes are _____.

5. Her date of birth is _____.

6. She is _____ years old.

B **Complete.**

1. His first name is _____.

2. His last name is _____.

3. His hair is _____.

4. His eyes are _____.

5. His date of birth is _____.

6. He is _____ years old.

C **Ask your partner the questions and complete the student ID card.**

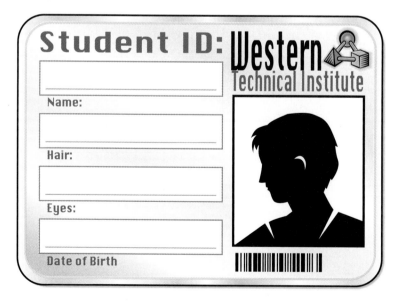

1. What is your first name?

2. What is your last name?

3. What color is your hair?

4. What color are your eyes?

5. What is your date of birth?

Am	I		Yes, you **are**.	No, you **aren't**.
Are	you		Yes, I **am**.	No, I'm **not**.
Is	he	tall?	Yes, he **is**.	No, he **isn't**.
	she		Yes, she **is**.	No, she **isn't**.
	it		Yes, it **is**.	No, it **isn't**.
Are	we		Yes, we **are**.	No, we **aren't**.
	they		Yes, they **are**.	No, they **aren't**.

A **Write the answer.**

1. Are you tall? _____

2. Are you young? _____

3. Are you from Mexico? _____

4. Is your hair black? _____

5. Is your hair blond? _____

6. Is your teacher from Canada? _____

7. Is he / she short? _____

8. Is he / she married? _____

B **Listen and write the questions.** Ask a partner the questions.

CD1·TR33

1. _____

2. _____

3. _____

4. _____

5. _____

Read about Anita. Then, ask and answer the questions with a partner.

This is my wife, Anita. She is from India. She is 40 years old. She is short and thin. Her hair is black and straight. It's very long. I think she is beautiful.

> Is Anita married?
>
> Yes, she is.

1. Anita / married?

2. she / from Vietnam?

3. her hair / black?

4. she / tall?

5. she / 20 years old?

6. she / beautiful?

  Read about Tony. Then, ask and answer the questions with a partner.

This is my boyfriend, Tony. Tony is 20 years old. He's from Portugal. He's tall and average weight. He has brown hair. His hair is short and curly. Tony has a moustache. I think Tony is handsome.

> Is Tony old?
>
> No, he isn't.

1. Tony / old?

2. he / from Portugal?

3. Tony / single?

4. he / short?

5. he / heavy?

6. he / handsome?

  Working Together **Bring in photos of your family.** Talk about your family.

HELPFUL EXPRESSIONS
- That's a nice picture. Is that you?
- Who's that? He's tall.
- Is she your sister?
- Is he married? How old is he?

A **Work with a partner.** Write two adjectives for each person in the picture.

Bob: _____ tall, bald _____

Sarah: _____

Linda: _____

Steve: _____

 B **Listen.** Write the names on the picture.

CD1·TR34

    Emily   Kim   Joanne   Mary   Andy

 C **Listen again.** Write the ages on the picture.

CD1·TR34

D **Complete.**

1. _____Mary_____ is tall and thin. She has short, curly hair.

2. _____ has a moustache, and he's bald.

3. _____ is 5 years old. She has long hair.

4. _____ is short and heavy. He has blond hair.

5. _____ is thin. She has straight, black hair.

6. _____ is tall and thin. He has curly hair.

7. _____ is tall and heavy. She has short, curly hair.

E **Answer the questions.** Then, ask and answer questions about the other people in this family.

Andy

1. How old is Andy?

2. Is he short?

3. Is he heavy?

4. What color is his hair?

5. Is it curly?

Mary

1. How old is Mary?

2. Is she single?

3. Is she tall?

4. What color is her hair?

5. Is it long?

F **Pronunciation: Statements and Questions** **Listen and repeat.**

CD1·TR35

Statements

1. He is tall.

2. She is short.

3. It is curly.

Questions

Is he tall?

Is she short?

Is it curly?

G **Listen and complete.** Then, put a period (.) or a question mark (?) at the end of each sentence.

CD1·TR36

1. ___She is___ old .

2. _____ young _

3. _____ heavy _

4. _____ tall _

5. _____ thin _

6. _____ tall _

7. _____ short _

8. _____ heavy _

H **Practice the sentences with a partner.**

 A Discuss.

1. How many people are in your family? What are their names?

2. Tell about the members of your family. Do they have children? Are they married, single, or divorced?

B Read.

Three Families

The Soto Family

This is my family. I live with my husband and our three children. My parents live in the same town. We see them every week. My husband's parents live four hours from here. We visit them on holidays and in the summer.

The Park Family

This is my family. I live with my wife and two children. My son is 10 and my daughter is 15. My parents live with us. They are both 70 years old, and they are retired.

The Taylor Family

This is my family. My husband and I are divorced, so I am a single mother. I have two children, a boy and a girl. They live with me, and they see their father every Saturday.

C Check (✔) the information that is true about each family.

	Sotos	Parks	Taylors
1. There are three children in this family.	✔		
2. The children live with their parents and grandparents.			
3. The parents are divorced.			
4. The children see their grandparents every week.			
5. The children do not see their father every day.			
6. There are six people in this family.			

D Circle the picture of the writer in each paragraph.

A **Read.**

> ## My Family
> My name is Liudmila. This is a photograph of my family. I am from Cuba. I have long, straight hair. My eyes are brown. This is my husband, Carlos. He is from Ecuador. Carlos is 30 years old. His hair is black. It's short and wavy. He is tall and handsome. This is our son. His name is Jake. He is very friendly. He has brown hair, and his eyes are brown, too. I think he looks like my husband.

B **Write about your family.** Bring in a photo. Who are the people in the photo? Describe what they look like.

My name is _____. This is a picture of _____

_____

_____

_____

C **Sharing Our Stories** **Read your partner's story.** Complete.

1. My partner is married / single / divorced.

2. My partner is from _____.

WRITING NOTE

A name begins with a capital letter.

Carlos

Marsha

Listen and repeat.

CD1·TR37

Months: January, February, March,
April, May, June,
July, August, September,
October, November, December

Days: Sunday, Monday, Tuesday,
Wednesday, Thursday, Friday, Saturday

  Listen and repeat.

CD1·TR38

Sunday	Monday	Tuesday	Wednesday	Thursday	Friday	Saturday
		1 first	2 second	3 third	4 fourth	5 fifth
6 sixth	7 seventh	8 eighth	9 ninth	10 tenth	11 eleventh	12 twelfth
13 thirteenth	14 fourteenth	15 fifteenth	16 sixteenth	17 seventeenth	18 eighteenth	19 nineteenth
20 twentieth	21 twenty-first	22 twenty-second	23 twenty-third	24 twenty-fourth	25 twenty-fifth	26 twenty-sixth
27 twenty-seventh	28 twenty-eighth	29 twenty-ninth	30 thirtieth	31 thirty-first		

WRITING NOTE

Months and days of the week begin with a capital letter.

January February

Monday Tuesday

 C **Listen and write.**

CD1·TR39

1. January 4, 2005

2. _____

3. _____   6. _____

4. _____   7. _____

5. _____   8. _____

  Practice saying the dates with a partner.

E **Read and complete.**

Date of birth: __9__ / __14__ / __75__
Month Day Year

Birth date: [ ][ ][ ][ ][ ][ ]
Month   Day   Year

1. **A:** What's your date of birth?
   B: September 14, 1975.
2. **A:** What's your date of birth?
   B: March 3, 1994.

F **Complete.**

Name: _____   _____   _____
         first   last   middle initial

Status: single   married   divorced   **Sex:**   male   female

Telephone: (   ) _____

Date of Birth: _____ _____ _____
                 month   day   year

NAME (Last, First, Middle)

MARITAL STATUS	SEX
Single Married Divorced	☐ Male ☐ Female
TELEPHONE NUMBER (include Area Code) ( )	BIRTH DATE Month / Day / Year _____ / _____ / _____

G **Answer the questions with a partner.**

1. Your aunt was born in 1980. How old is she? _____
2. Your mother was born in 1962. How old is she? _____
3. How old is your grandfather? He was born in 1940. _____
4. Your father is 40 years old. What year was he born? _____
5. Your brother is 18. What year was he born? _____

Unit 4

At Home

Rooms, Furniture, and Appliances

 A Listen and repeat.

CD1·TR40

Rooms

1. a living room

2. a dining room

3. a kitchen

4. a bathroom

5. a bedroom

Furniture and Appliances

1. a sofa

2. a coffee table

3. an armchair

4. pillows

5. an end table

6. a lamp

7. a TV

8. a fireplace

9. a bookcase

10. a picture

11. a rug

12. a mirror

 **13.** a bed

 **14.** a dresser

 **15.** a night table

 **16.** a desk

 17. a window

 **18.** a dining table

 19. a chair

 20. a cabinet

 21. a stove

 **22.** a sink

 **23.** a microwave

 24. a refrigerator

 **25.** a closet

 26. a toilet

 **27.** a bathtub

 **28.** a shower

WORD PARTNERSHIPS	
make	the bed
take	a bath a shower
turn on turn off	the TV the lamp the microwave the washer

A **Look at the floor plan.** Complete the sentences.

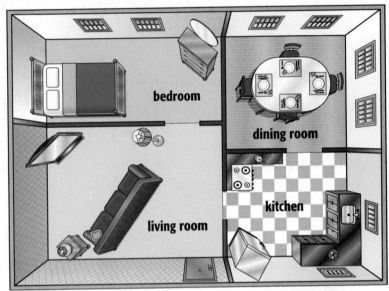

1. There is a sofa in the _____living room_____.

2. There is a bed in the _____.

3. There are four chairs in the _____.

4. There is a TV in the _____.

5. There is a refrigerator in the _____.

B **Write four more sentences about the floor plan.**

1. There is an end table in the living room._____

2. _____

3. _____

4. _____

5. _____

C **Working Together** **Draw a floor plan of your home.** Talk about your home.

> I have a TV in my bedroom.

> There is a TV in my bedroom, too.

A **Listen and repeat.**

CD1·TR41

The book is **on** the chair.
The lamp is **next to** the chair.

The book is **under** the chair.

The window is **in back of** the chair.
The chair is **in front of** the window.

The book is **between** the chair and the desk.

The book is **in** the desk.

The picture is **above** the chair.
The picture is **over** the chair.

B **Complete.**

1. book

2. mirror

3. picture

4. lamp

5. night table

6. picture

1. The book is ___under___ the coffee table.

2. The mirror is _____ the dresser.

3. The picture is _____ the desk.

4. The lamp is _____ the armchair and the sofa.

5. The night table is _____ the bed.

6. The picture is _____ the closet.

Where	is	the book?
	are	the books?

It	is	on the desk.
They	are	

It is = It's
They are = They're

 A **Listen and write each question.** Then, look at the picture and write the answer.

CD1·TR42

1. **Q:** Where is the end table?

   A: It's next to the armchair.

2. **Q:** _____

   A: _____

3. **Q:** _____

   A: _____

4. **Q:** _____

   A: _____

5. **Q:** _____

   A: _____

6. **Q:** _____

   A: _____

B **Working Together** **Work in a group.** Put objects on a desk. Talk about their location. Then, move the objects around. Talk about their new location.

> The cell phone is on the table.

> Now the cell phone is under the table.

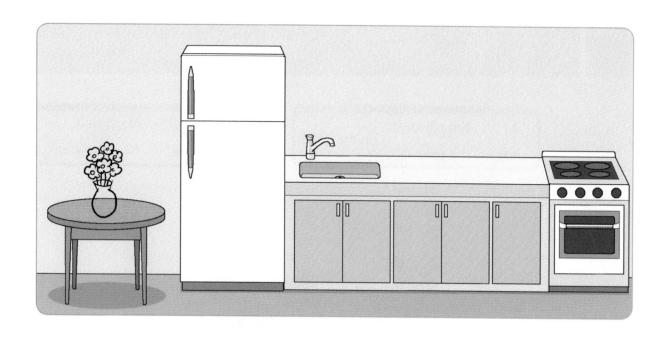

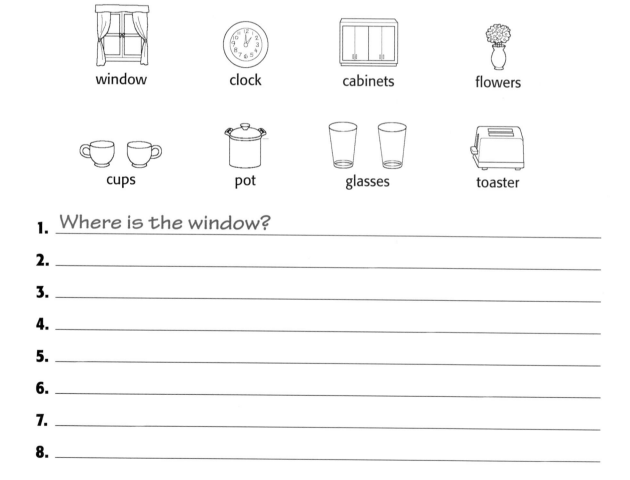

Working Together **Draw the following objects in your kitchen.** Write eight questions. Ask your partner each question.

window	clock	cabinets	flowers
cups	pot	glasses	toaster

1. Where is the window? _____

2. _____

3. _____

4. _____

5. _____

6. _____

7. _____

8. _____

Is	the pillow	on the sofa?
Are	the pillows	

Yes, it is.	No, it isn't.
Yes, they are.	No, they aren't.

A **Look at the picture.** Answer.

1. A: Is the computer on the desk?　　**B:** _____Yes, it is._____

2. A: Is the lamp next to the armchair?　　**B:** _____

3. A: Are the books on the coffee table?　　**B:** _____

4. A: Is the end table between the sofa and the armchair?　　**B:** _____

5. A: Is the desk under the window?　　**B:** _____

6. A: Is the armchair next to the end table?　　**B:** _____

7. A: Are the pillows on the armchair?　　**B:** _____

8. A: Is the coffee table in front of the sofa?　　**B:** _____

B **Work with a partner.** Ask and answer questions about the people and things in the picture.

1. the flowers   3. the window   5. the woman

2. the cat   4. the man   6. the sofa

C **Look at the picture on page 50 and listen to the conversation.** Write the missing questions.

CD1·TR43

Tom: Where is my cell phone?

Sara: _Is it on the coffee table?_

Tom: No, it isn't.

Sara: _____

Tom: No, it isn't.

Sara: _____

Tom: Yes, here it is!

D **Listen.** Write the missing questions.

CD1·TR44

Tom: Where are my keys?

Sara: _____

Tom: No, they aren't.

Sara: _____

Tom: No, they aren't.

Tom: Are they on the desk?

Sara: Yes, here they are!

E **Working Together** **Work with a partner.** Look at page 50. Act out a conversation with these items: glasses, camera, and cat.

The Big Picture

A Write the name of each object.

bed	~~CDs~~	dresser	computer	night table	printer
TV	clothes	bookcase	remote	stereo	telephone

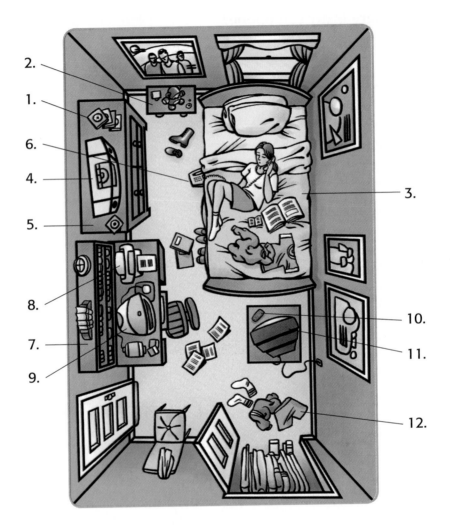

1.	CDs	5.	_____	9.	_____
2.	_____	6.	_____	10.	_____
3.	_____	7.	_____	11.	_____
4.	_____	8.	_____	12.	_____

  B Listen.

CD1·TR45

🔊 **C** **Listen to the questions.** Write the number of the question next to Kathy's answer.

_____ **a.** "Mom, my clothes are in the closet."

_____ **b.** "Mom, my books and papers are on the desk."

_____ **c.** "Yes, Mom. My room is perfect."

_____1_____ **d.** "Yes, I have a lot of homework."

_____ **e.** "They're in the closet."

D **Complete each sentence with the correct preposition.**

1. The pillows are _____ on _____ the bed.

2. The stereo is _____ the dresser.

3. The CDs are _____ the stereo.

4. The computer is _____ the desk.

5. The printer is _____ the computer.

6. Some clothes are _____ the closet.

7. The telephone is _____ the bed.

👥 **E** **Ask and answer the questions.**

1. Is the desk next to the bed?

2. Is the window over the bed?   No, it isn't.

3. Are the pillows on the floor?

4. Is the TV on the dresser?

5. Are the shoes under the bed?

6. Are the clothes on the bed?

7. Is the remote under the chair?

8. Is Kathy on her bed?

> Yes, it is.
> No, it isn't.
> Yes, they are.
> No, they aren't.
> Yes, she is.
> No, she isn't.

👥 **F** **Ask and answer questions about things in Kathy's room.**

Where are her shoes?

They're under the bed.

Reading

 **A** **Discuss.**

1. What is the name of your local newspaper?

2. Where is the classified ad section?

B **Read.**

Garage Sales

In your local newspaper, you can find ads for garage sales, yard sales, or tag sales in your area. At these sales, you can buy furniture, electronic equipment, children's items, clothing, and kitchen items at very good prices.

1 CLARK	**3 CRANFORD**	**5 FANWOOD**	**7 PLAINFIELD**
16 Poplar Drive – **Saturday 9am-3pm.** Sofa, girl's bedroom set, kitchen table, kitchen items. Rain or shine.	**55 Holly Street** – Moving to Florida! **Saturday 8am-6pm.** Lots of furniture! Beds, dressers, night tables, chairs, sofa, end tables, dining room set, TV.	**33 West End Avenue** – Three Family Garage Sale. **Saturday 9-4.** Dishes, kitchen items, books, clothing, refrigerator, microwave.	**377 Raritan Road –** **Saturday 9-4.** Neighborhood Garage Sale! Furniture, pictures, rugs, mirrors, lamps, stereo and CDs, kitchen items.
2 CLARK	**4 CRANFORD**	**6 GARWOOD**	**8 SUMMIT**
32 Standish Way – **Friday and Saturday** **10am-5pm.** Baby items, car seat, lots of toys and clothing.	**456 Willow Street –** **Friday 9 to 5.** Something for everyone. Lots of electronic equipment – computer, stereo, telephones, printer.	**472 Summit Avenue –** **Friday and Saturday 9-3.** Moving sale. Twin beds, 2 sofas, washing machine and dryer, bookcase and books, chairs, coffee table, lamps, and much more!	**44 North Avenue –** **Friday and Saturday** **9am-3pm.** Lots of kitchen items – dishwasher, microwave, small refrigerator, dishes, cups, glasses, pots, and lots more!

C **Circle these items in the ads.**

1. a refrigerator   3. a TV   5. kitchen items   7. bedroom furniture

2. baby items   4. a sofa   6. a printer   8. a microwave

  D **Working Together** **Go online and look at a website with classified ads.** Or, bring in the classified section of your local newspaper. Circle the garage sales that you want to visit.

A **Read.**

> I live in an apartment in San Diego. My wife and children are in Poland, so I live alone. My apartment has a bedroom and a small kitchen. There is a refrigerator, a microwave, and a table in the kitchen. I have an armchair and a TV. I have a bed and a dresser. My apartment is small, but it's the right size for me.

> I live in a house in Chicago. It has six rooms. There are three bedrooms and two bathrooms. The living room is on the first floor. There is a TV and a computer in the living room. My house is very big and it has a backyard. I need a big house because I have three children.

> **WRITING NOTE**
> The names of cities begin with capital letters:
> San Francisco

B **Check the information that is true for you.**

☐ I live in a house.

☐ I live in an apartment.

☐ I live alone.

☐ I live with _____.

☐ There are _____ rooms.

☐ I have a small _____.

☐ I have a large _____.

☐ There's a TV in my bedroom.

C **Write about your home.**

_____

_____

D **Sharing Our Stories** **Read your partner's story.** **Complete the sentences.**

My partner lives in _____. It has _____ rooms.

English in Action

A Read.

A: What's your address?

B: 419 South Avenue.

A: And the town?

B: Cranford.

A: What's your zip code?

B: 07016.

South Avenue

  B **Listen to each address and repeat.**

CD1 · TR47

  C **Listen.** Complete the addresses. Then, repeat the addresses with a partner.

CD1 · TR48

a. _____ North Avenue

b. _____ Maple Street

c. _____ Central Avenue

d. _____ Park Avenue

e. _____ Second Street

f. _____ Main Street

  D **Working Together** **Interview three students.** Complete the chart.

	What's your name?	**What's your address?**	**What's your zip code?**
1.			
2.			
3.			

A **Read.** What information is on each line?

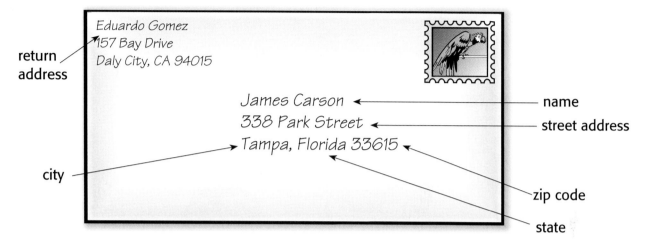

return address
city
name
street address
zip code
state

Eduardo Gomez
157 Bay Drive
Daly City, CA 94015

James Carson
338 Park Street
Tampa, Florida 33615

B **Circle** the problems.

Marco Martinez
893 Hudson
Lansing Mishigan

Charles Madison
34 10 street
Lansing Mishigan

U.S. POSTAGE

C **Address this envelope to the President of the United States.** The address is 1600 Pennsylvania Avenue NW, Washington, D.C. 20500. Remember to write your return address.

I'm Talking on the Phone

Dictionary

Actions

A **Listen and repeat.**

CD2·TR1

1. He is eating.

2. She is washing the car.

3. She is listening to music.

4. They are studying.

5. He is cooking.

6. She is sleeping.

7. He is reading.

8. She is drinking.

9. They are talking.

10. They are watching TV.

11. He is doing his homework.

12. She is cleaning the house.

13. She is driving.

14. They are walking.

15. She is making lunch.

16. He is doing the laundry.

Word Builder

A Complete.

is reading	is talking	are watching	~~is cooking~~	is sleeping
are studying	am writing	is drinking	is eating	are listening

1. She _____ is cooking _____ dinner.

2. She _____ the newspaper.

3. I _____ in my notebook.

4. They _____ a movie.

5. The students _____ English.

6. He's in bed. He _____.

7. She _____ a cup of coffee.

8. They _____ to the stereo.

9. He _____ on the telephone.

10. He _____ a hamburger.

WORD PARTNERSHIPS	
make	dinner
	the bed
	a phone call
do	homework
	the dishes
	laundry

B Working Together **Act out an activity.** The class will guess the action.

> You are eating.

> You are dancing.

C Write six new actions on the lines.

1. _____

2. _____

3. _____

4. _____

5. _____

6. _____

D Write three more sentences about the people in your family. What is each person doing now? Read your sentences to another student.

1. My mother is working. _____

2. _____

3. _____

4. _____

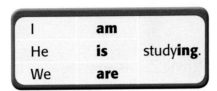

I	am	
He	is	study**ing**.
We	are	

A **Complete the sentences.**

1. I'm at school. I ___am studying___ English. (study)

2. Maria is at the store. She _____ a notebook. (buy)

3. The students are at the library. They _____ for a test. (study)

4. The baby is in his bedroom. He _____. (sleep)

5. You are on the phone. You _____ to your friend. (talk)

6. Jason is in the kitchen. He _____ dinner. (make)

7. Larry is in his car. He _____ to work. (drive)

8. We _____ in the classroom. (sit)

B **Pronunciation: Contractions** **Listen and repeat the sentences.**

CD2·TR2

Long Forms	**Contractions**
1. I am studying.	I'm studying.
2. She is reading.	She's reading.
3. He is sleeping.	He's sleeping.
4. We are talking.	We're talking.
5. They are eating.	They're eating.
6. You are cooking.	You're cooking.

C **Listen and (circle) the form you hear.**

CD2·TR3

1. **a.** He is walking.
   b. He's walking.

2. **a.** She is cleaning.
   b. She's cleaning.

3. **a.** I am making lunch.
   b. I'm making lunch.

4. **a.** You are driving.
   b. You're driving.

5. **a.** They are watching TV.
   b. They're watching TV.

6. **a.** We are studying.
   b. We're studying.

D Read. Underline the verbs in the present continuous.

It is Saturday morning, and everyone in the Lee family is busy. Jenny is in the bathroom. She's <u>taking</u> a shower. Jenny is getting ready for work. David is in his bedroom. He's sitting at his desk and studying for a test on Monday. Mrs. Lee is in the living room. She's cleaning. Right now, she's vacuuming the rug. Mr. Lee is in the kitchen. He's cooking lunch for the family. Carla is helping. She's washing the dishes. Grandma Lee is in the kitchen, too. She's doing the laundry.

E Match.

____d____ **1.** Where is Jenny?   **a.** She's in the living room.

_____ **2.** What is she doing?   **b.** He's cooking lunch.

_____ **3.** Where is Mrs. Lee?   **c.** He's studying.

_____ **4.** What is she doing?   **d.** She's in the bathroom.

_____ **5.** Where is Mr. Lee?   **e.** She's cleaning.

_____ **6.** What is he doing?   **f.** She's taking a shower.

_____ **7.** Where is David?   **g.** He's in the kitchen.

_____ **8.** What is he doing?   **h.** He's in his bedroom.

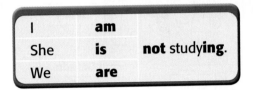

I	am	
She	is	**not** study**ing**.
We	are	

A **Use the words to talk about yourself and your class.** Some sentences are
affirmative and some sentences are negative.

1. I / study / French

2. I / talk / on my cell phone I'm not studying French.

3. We / sit / in class

4. I / look at / page 25

5. We / watch / TV

6. I / wear / a hat

7. The teacher / drink / a cup of coffee

8. The students / sit / at their desks

B **Complete the sentences.** Some sentences are negative and some are affirmative.

1. Mariana _isn't studying_ at home. (study)

2. She _____ in the library. (study)

3. She _____ a cup of coffee. (drink)

4. She _____ in her notebook. (write)

5. They _____ the dishes. (do)

6. They _____ the laundry. (do)

7. They _____ TV. (watch)

8. They _____ about school. (talk)

Question	Short Answers	
Are you work**ing**?	Yes, I **am**.	No, **I'm not**.
Is she work**ing**?	Yes, she **is**.	No, she **isn't**.
Are they work**ing**?	Yes, they **are**.	No, they **aren't**.

A **Answer the questions with a partner.**

Yes, she is.

1. Is she cleaning her house?

2. Is she washing her car?

3. Is she listening to music?

4. Is she doing the laundry?

B **Answer the questions with a partner.**

1. Are they sitting on the sofa?

2. Are they eating dinner?

3. Are they watching TV?

4. Are they talking?

C **Work with a partner.** Ask and answer the questions.

1. Are you sitting in class?

2. Are you writing?

3. Are you drinking a soda?

4. Are you talking?

5. Are you listening to music?

6. Are you speaking English?

D **Complete with *is* or *are*.**

1. __Is__ the student sleeping?

2. _____ the boys playing soccer?

3. _____ the students walking to school?

4. _____ Michael reading a book?

5. _____ Serena writing a letter?

6. _____ the men working?

7. _____ your sister studying English?

8. _____ you doing your homework?

I'm on the phone

 A **Listen and complete.**

CD2·TR4

A: Hello.

B: Hi, Jenny. It's Sarah. Where are you?

A: _____.

B: What are you doing?

A: _____.

B: Okay. I'll call you later.

> **When making a phone call, say your name.**
>
> "Hi. This is Maria."
> "Hi. It's Maria."

 B **Listen and complete.**

CD2·TR5

A: Hello.

B: Hi, Alex. It's Ben. _____?

A: I'm at work.

B: _____?

A: I'm writing a report.

B: Okay. I'll call you later.

C **Working Together** **Choose one of the pictures.** Write a conversation with a partner. Act out your conversation for the class.

A: Hello. _____ _____.

B: Hi, _____. It's _____. Where are you?

A: _____.

B: What are you doing?

A: _____.

B: Okay. I'll call you later.

 A Working Together **In a group, look at the picture of this family.** Name each person and write about them. Where are they? What are they doing?

B Working Together **Work in a group.** Choose two places from the locations below. What are people doing? Write four sentences. Use your imagination.

park   cafeteria   student lounge   airplane

computer lab   bus   office   car

Example: car

1. A man is driving.

2. A woman is listening to the radio.

3. A driver is stopping at the red light.

4. A man is talking on his cell phone.

A **Listen to the conversation between Tommy and his mother.**

CD2·TR6

B **Listen again and write the names on the picture.**

CD2·TR6

Mom   Tommy   Brian   Katie   Dad

C **Complete.**

1. Tommy is in the _kitchen_ .

2. Brian is in the _____ .

3. Katie is in her _____ .

4. Dad is in the _____ .

5. Mom is at _____ .

🔊 **D** **Listen and write short answers.**

CD2·TR7

1. No, she isn't.

2. _____

3. _____

4. _____

5. _____

6. _____

7. _____

> Yes, he is.
> No, he isn't.
> Yes, she is.
> No, she isn't.

E **Match.**

_____b_____ **1.** Where is Tommy?   **a.** No, he isn't.

_____ **2.** What is he doing?   **b.** He's in the kitchen.

_____ **3.** Is Tommy playing video games?   **c.** He's playing video games.

_____ **4.** Is Tommy talking to his mother?   **d.** He's watching TV.

_____ **5.** Where is Brian?   **e.** No, he isn't.

_____ **6.** What is he doing?   **f.** Yes, he is.

_____ **7.** Is Brian sleeping?   **g.** He's in the living room.

F **Answer.**

1. Where is Dad? He's in the living room. _____

2. Is he cooking dinner? _____

3. What's he doing? _____

4. Where is Katie? _____

5. What's she doing? _____

6. Is she doing her homework? _____

👥 **G** **Working Together** **Work with another student.** Write a conversation between the mother and the father.

Reading

A Read.

Everybody's Talking

On the street, people are walking and talking on their cell phones. In cars, people are driving and talking. In offices, people are working and talking on the phone.

Finland was the first country in the world with cell phones. The largest cell phone company in the world is in Finland. Now, there are more than four billion cell phones in the world. China has more cell phones than any other country. In many countries, there are more cell phones than people. For example, there are more cell phones than people in Hong Kong and Portugal. Many people have two cell phones, one for home and one for work. People use their cell phones for many things. They play games, listen to music, take photographs, and use the Internet. In Japan, people are using cell phones to learn English.

Teachers are not happy about cell phones. When they are teaching, cell phones ring. Sometimes, students text message each other. They text message one another during tests! In many schools, students cannot bring their cell phones to class. In other schools, students must turn off their cell phones before class.

B Match.

_____ **1.** Finland   **a.** This country has more cell phones than any other country.

_____ **2.** Portugal   **b.** Many people in this country get English lessons on their phones.

_____ **3.** China   **c.** This country has more cell phones than people.

_____ **4.** Japan   **d.** This country is the home of the largest cell phone company.

 C **Talk about the rules for using cell phones at your school.** What is the policy in your school? Can you bring cell phones to your class?

Writing Our Stories

A Read.

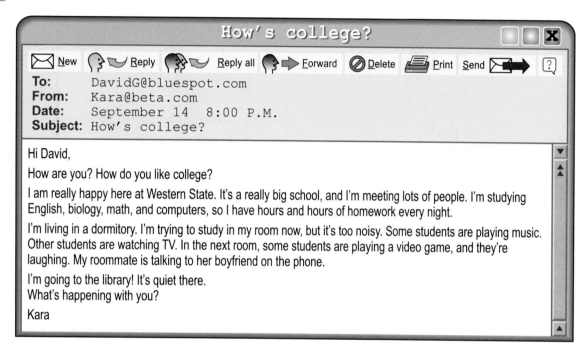

How's college?

New | Reply | Reply all | Forward | Delete | Print | Send | ?

To: DavidG@bluespot.com
From: Kara@beta.com
Date: September 14 8:00 P.M.
Subject: How's college?

Hi David,

How are you? How do you like college?

I am really happy here at Western State. It's a really big school, and I'm meeting lots of people. I'm studying English, biology, math, and computers, so I have hours and hours of homework every night.

I'm living in a dormitory. I'm trying to study in my room now, but it's too noisy. Some students are playing music. Other students are watching TV. In the next room, some students are playing a video game, and they're laughing. My roommate is talking to her boyfriend on the phone.

I'm going to the library! It's quiet there.
What's happening with you?

Kara

> **WRITING NOTE**
>
> Use a spell check before sending e-mail.

B Write an e-mail to a friend. What are you doing now?

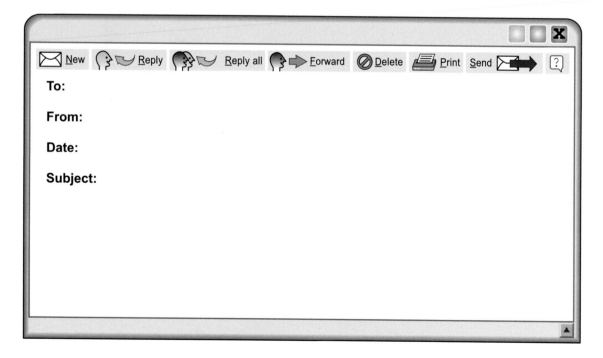

New | Reply | Reply all | Forward | Delete | Print | Send | ?

To:

From:

Date:

Subject:

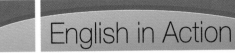

CD2·TR8

A **Listen and look at the message.**

Call
Steve Carson
555-8341

TELEPHONE EXPRESSIONS

This is _____.
May I speak to _____?
Can I take a message?
Please ask him/her to call me.
Please repeat that.

CD2·TR9

B **Listen to two phone calls.** Take the messages.

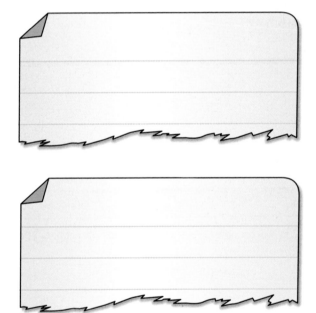

 C **Working Together** **Work with a partner.** Write and practice leaving a message. Act out your conversation for the class.

 D **Working Together** **Take your cell phone outside the classroom.** Call another student in class, and leave a short message.

179 Palmer – Park

Palmer David 177 Central Av Cranford......................555-1483	Pannullo T 46 Sussex St Plainfield............................555-4316
Palmer Emily 43 Grand St Cranford........................555-1234	Panosh John 336 Forest Ave Westfield.....................555-8274
Palmer R 34 Broad St Essex....................................555-5477	Pantagis Stephen 3 Chester Ave Essex.....................555-8682
Palmer William 6 Linden L Fanwood......................555-6134	Pantagis Susan 200 Broad St Fanwood.....................555-8833
Palmieri Ann 45 Grove St Fanwood........................555-5579	Pantano N 59 Maple St Plainfield.............................555-7604
Palmieri Fred 114 Maple T Essex............................555-9966	Pantoja R 80 Prospect St Essex................................555-9038
Palumbo Ed 110 South Ave Warrenville...................555-1024	Paoli P 621 Sunny Drive Plainfield...........................555-8652
Palumbo George 110 South Av Essex.......................555-6403	Paolo Stephen 56 Davis Rd Plainfield.......................555-0294
Palumbo Henry 184 Second St Essex........................555-4403	Paone Joan 44 Harding St Essex...............................555-5657
Palumbo L 23 Coles Way Fanwood..........................555-7761	Papa's Pizza 77 Main St Plainfield............................555-2534
Palumbo P 650 Brant Crt Cranford...........................555-7463	Papen Chris 204 Euclid Av Plainfield........................555-8541
Palusci Ellen 67 Main St Warrenville.......................555-9832	Papen George 399 Glen Road Fanwood....................555-2538
Palusci Martin 173 First St Essex..............................555-4411	Papen Theresa 75 Glen Road Fanwood.....................555-7520
Panagos Cleaners 43 South Ave Essex......................555-7764	Papik B 34 Hazel Court Warrenville...........................555-6852
Panagos H 65 Rahway Rd Fanwood.........................555-0102	Pappas John and Marge 12 Lake Ave Essex...........555-6427
Panagos Joseph 76 Third Av Fanwood.....................555-2310	Pappas S 216 State St Plainfield................................555-0208
Panarese B 876 Park Av Warrenville.........................555-8525	Parada Juan 169 Sunset St Plainfield.........................555-7314
Panarese Brad 9 Willow Ave Cranford......................555-0113	Parada Ricardo 14 Forest Ave Essex..........................555-6291
Panarese C 453 Rogers Way Essex............................555-7509	Parada Teresa 90 South Av Cranford.........................555-7326
Panasik Craig 65 Davis Road Fanwood.....................555-8029	Paradise Ed 501 Martin St Fanwood..........................555-6491
Panek Darren 431 Coles Way Essex..........................555-7435	Paradise H 36 Grant Av Essex...................................555-2509
Panek Katherine 107 Charles St Fanwood................555-1128	Pardo Charles 153 Glen Road Fanwood....................555-8574
Panek Bakery 54 Center St Cranford.........................555-7039	Pardon R 54 Paulis St Warrenville.............................555-2530
Panera Richard 87 Route 22 Cranford.......................555-2085	Parente A 591 Hort St Warrenville.............................555-0203
Pang Hang 43 Grove Av Fanwood............................555-6965	Parente E 88 Broad St Westield.................................555-8637
Pang J 44 Thomas St Plainfield.................................555-7413	Parisi L 71 Francis Av Plainfield................................555-8630
Pang Y 87 Woods Way Plainfield..............................555-8530	Parisi M 490 Kent Place Plainfield.............................555-3250
Pango L 866 Baker St Plainfield................................555-2527	Park In-Chui 937 North Av Fanwood.........................555-7831
Pannone 60 Davis Rd Fanwood................................555-4682	Park Jeong 503 Lake Av Cranford.............................555-1509

A Write the phone numbers.

Emily Palmer _____ John and Marge Pappas _____

Y Pang _____ Henry Palumbo _____

Juan Parada _____ Charles Pardo _____

B Write the addresses.

Papa's Pizza _____

Panagos Cleaners _____

Jeong Park _____

Unit

6 My City

Dictionary
Adjectives, Locations, Weather

CD2·TR10

A **Listen and repeat.**

Adjectives

1. large

2. small

3. quiet

4. noisy

5. busy

6. clean

7. dirty

8. fun

9. safe

10. dangerous

11. beautiful

12. ugly

13. cheap

14. expensive

15. interesting

16. boring

17. heavy

18. light

19. friendly

20. unfriendly

CD2·TR11 **B** **Listen and repeat.**

Locations

4. on the border

5. in the north

2. in the mountains

8. in the east

1. in the west

6. in the center
7. in the middle

9. the capital ★

3. in the desert

10. near the ocean

11. in the south

CD2·TR12 **C** **Listen and repeat.**

Weather

1. wet / rainy

2. dry

3. humid

4. hot

5. cold / snowy

Word Builder

A Match the opposites.

_____h_____	**1.** busy	**a.**	ugly
_____	**2.** wet	**b.**	expensive
_____	**3.** clean	**c.**	unfriendly
_____	**4.** quiet	**d.**	boring
_____	**5.** cheap	**e.**	light
_____	**6.** beautiful	**f.**	noisy
_____	**7.** interesting	**g.**	dry
_____	**8.** small	**h.**	quiet
_____	**9.** friendly	**i.**	dirty
_____	**10.** heavy	**j.**	large

B Circle the adjectives.

1. The city where I live is **beautiful / ugly**.

2. It is **interesting / boring**.

3. My building is **small / large**.

4. My neighborhood is **busy / quiet**.

5. The streets are **clean / dirty**.

6. The traffic near my house is **heavy / light**.

7. The people are **friendly / unfriendly** to visitors.

8. Today the weather is **hot / cold / and wet / dry**.

WORD PARTNERSHIPS	
a busy	neighborhood
a convenient	
a friendly	neighbor
a helpful	

Working Together **With a group of students, label the states on the map.**

Seattle <u>Washington</u>

Boston _____

Detroit _____

Chicago _____

New York _____

San Francisco _____

Las Vegas _____

Phoenix _____

San Antonio _____

Miami _____

Arizona	Florida	Massachusetts	Nevada	Texas
California	Illinois	Michigan	New York	~~Washington~~

 D **Listen and point to each city on the map.** Listen again and repeat.

CD2·TR13

E **Read and circle.**

1. Seattle is in the east.   True   (False)

2. San Francisco is near the ocean.   True   False

3. Miami is in the mountains.   True   False

4. Phoenix is in the desert.   True   False

5. Detroit is near Canada.   True   False

6. Chicago is in the east.   True   False

7. San Antonio is in the middle of the U.S.   True   False

8. Boston is in the east.   True   False

9. New York is in the west.   True   False

10. The border between the U.S. and Canada is very long.   True   False

 A **Ask and answer questions about the city where you study.**

Is	New York	small		large?
Are	the streets	clean	**or**	dirty?

1. Is this city small or large?

2. Are the people friendly or unfriendly?

3. Is it quiet or noisy?

4. Is the weather dry or humid?

5. Is the weather hot, cold, or warm?

6. Is shopping for food cheap or expensive?

7. Are the streets busy or quiet?

8. _____?

> Is this city small or large?

> It's small.

> Are the people friendly or unfriendly?

> They're friendly.

 B **Working Together** **Work with a partner.** Ask and answer questions about your hometown.

> Is your hometown quiet?

> Yes, it is.

> Is your hometown noisy?

> No, it isn't.

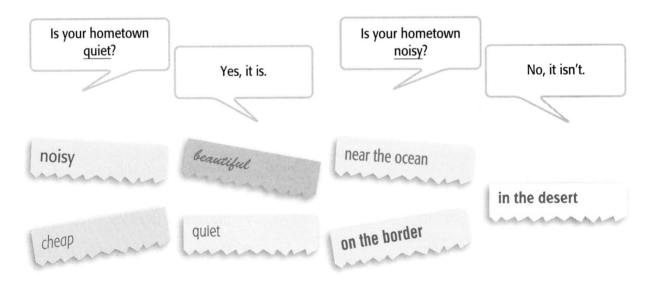

noisy

beautiful

near the ocean

in the desert

cheap

quiet

on the border

 C **Dictation** **Work with a partner.**

Student 1: Turn to page 226 and read Questions 1–6 to your partner.

Student 2: Listen and write your answers. Then, turn to page 227 and read Questions 7–12 to your partner.

A **Listen and complete.**

CD2·TR14

> I want to visit Beijing **because** it's interesting.
> They want to visit Brazil **because** the beaches are beautiful.

A: What city do you want to visit?

B: I want to visit _____Miami_____.

A: Why do you want to go there?

B: I want to visit Miami because it's _____.

A: Well, *I* want to visit _____.

B: Why do you want to go there?

A: Because it's _____. There are so many things to do!

  B **Working Together** **Talk about a city you want to visit.** Agree on a place to go.

> Where do you want to go?

> I want to visit Paris.

> Really? Why do you want to go there?

> I want to see Paris because it's a beautiful city.

> **Put the adjective before the noun.**
>
> This is a **large city.**
> New York is a **large city.**
> Boston and Chicago are **large cities.**
> Tampa is near a **beautiful beach.**
> Miami is near **beautiful beaches.**

> **Do not put an 's' on an adjective.**
>
> Miami is near beautiful~~s~~ beaches.

A **Complete the sentences.** Use a singular or plural noun.

1. There are friendly _____ students _____ at our school.

2. There is an old _____ in our classroom.

3. There are cheap _____ in this city.

4. There is an interesting _____ in this city.

5. There is a fun _____ in this city.

6. There are noisy _____ in this city.

7. There is an ugly _____ in this city.

B **Working Together** **With your group, complete the sentences.** Use an adjective.

1. We are _____ students.

2. We have _____ books.

3. We study in a / an _____ classroom.

4. English is a / an _____ language.

5. We have _____ desks.

6. Our school is in a / an _____ area.

7. We have a / an _____ teacher.

8. We like the _____ weather in our city, but we don't like

   the _____ weather.

> We are friendly students.

Write the sentences in the correct order.

1. there / beaches / in this city / beautiful / are

   <u>There are beautiful beaches in this city.</u>

2. fun / is / a / there / park / in my area

   _____

3. is / on this street / museum / there / interesting / an

   _____

4. buildings / there / in New York / are / tall

   _____

5. large / in the east / are / there / businesses

   _____

6. weather / in the mountains / there / cold / is / and snowy

   _____

Working Together **Make a short presentation.** Stand in front of the class. Talk about your hometown. Give the following information.

1. I am from _____, _____.
                      city   country

2. My city **is / is not** the capital of the country.

3. _____ is in the _____ of the country.
   city   location

4. The weather is _____.

The Big Picture

A **Can you identify these people and places?**

The Brookfield Zoo	Barack Obama	a blues club
The Art Institute of Chicago	Oprah Winfrey	Wrigley Field
Lake Michigan		

 B **Listen.**

CD2·TR15

C **Match.**

_____C_____ **1.** paintings   **a.** blues clubs

_____ **2.** musicians   **b.** Wrigley Field

_____ **3.** Oprah Winfrey   **c.** The Art Institute of Chicago

_____ **4.** baseball   **d.** The Brookfield Zoo

_____ **5.** animals   **e.** President of the United States

_____ **6.** Barack Obama   **f.** a large lake in the north

_____ **7.** Lake Michigan   **g.** a TV talk show host

D **Listen again and circle.**

CD2·TR15

1. Chicago is in the south of the United States.   True   False

2. Chicago is next to water.   True   False

3. Spring is a good time to visit Chicago.   True   False

4. Chicago's summers are hot.   True   False

5. There are many opportunities to see art and listen to music.   True   False

6. Chicago has one professional sports team.   True   False

7. Oprah Winfrey is a popular blues musician.   True   False

8. Barack Obama is originally from Chicago.   True   False

E **Work with a partner.** Ask and answer the questions.

1. Is Chicago in the midwest or in the south?

2. Are the winters in Chicago warm or cold?

3. Is Chicago near a lake or an ocean?

4. Is Chicago famous for rock music or blues music?

5. Is Wrigley Field a baseball field or a football field?

6. Is the Brookfield Zoo interesting or boring for children?

7. Is downtown Chicago quiet or busy?

> Is Chicago a city or a state?

> It's a city.

F **Complete with *is, isn't, are,* or *aren't*.**

1. It ___is___ fun to see professional sports in Chicago.

2. Lake Michigan _____ a large, beautiful lake.

3. Winters in Chicago _____ hot and humid.

4. Downtown Chicago _____ busy.

5. The Art Institute of Chicago _____ a boring museum.

6. The Brookfield Zoo _____ fun for children.

7. Chicago's blues clubs _____ exciting and fun.

A Discuss. Then read.

1. Look at the U.S. map on page 244. Where is Seattle, Washington?

2. Is Seattle near the mountains? Is it near an ocean?

Seattle

Seattle is the largest city in Washington State. The population of Seattle is 594,210. It is in the northwest of the United States. It is in a beautiful location near the Pacific Ocean and Canada. Seattle is a busy seaport. Boats come and go to many other seaports in the world.

Seattle is a beautiful city, but it is a wet city. It gets 36.2 inches (92 cm.) of rain every year. Between October and May, it is cloudy almost every day. When the weather is clear, you can see the famous volcano, Mount Rainier.

Many people know Seattle because of the Space Needle. You can take an elevator to the top and see the whole city. You can see the University of Washington and the seaport.

Seattle's Space Needle

There are many large companies in Seattle. One makes computer software and one makes coffee.

Seattle residents enjoy both college and professional sports. There is a professional baseball team, a women's basketball team, and a football team. Seattle is a good place to live and work, and it's a fun place to visit.

B Circle the answer.

1. Seattle is a large city.	True	False
2. Seattle is in the southwest of the United States.	True	False
3. Seattle has warm, sunny weather all year.	True	False
4. Many large companies are in Seattle.	True	False
5. Seattle is a good place for a vacation.	True	False

C Underline the adjectives in the reading.

Writing Our Stories

A Read.

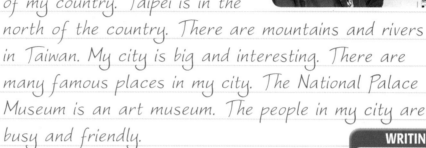

My name is Steven Lee. I am from Taipei, Taiwan. The population of my city is about 7,700,000. It is the capital of my country. Taipei is in the north of the country. There are mountains and rivers in Taiwan. My city is big and interesting. There are many famous places in my city. The National Palace Museum is an art museum. The people in my city are busy and friendly.

> **WRITING NOTE**
>
> Use a comma between the name of a city and the name of a country.
>
> Puebla, Mexico

B Write about your hometown.

My name is _____. I am from

_____, _____. The population of my
      city   country

city is about _____. It **is / is not** the capital city of my

country. _____ is in the _____ of the
             city   location

country. There are _____ in my city. My city is

_____ and _____. There are **many /**
   adjective   adjective

a few famous places in my city. _____

_____

C Sharing Our Stories Share your story with a partner. Complete.

1. My partner is from _____, _____.
                           city   country

2. The population of **his / her** city is _____.

3. My partner's city is _____ and _____.
                        adjective   adjective

A **Look at the map and complete the sentences.**

Sacramento

San Francisco

San José

Los Angeles

San Diego

Nevada

Arizona

Mexico

Oregon

Pacific Ocean

1. The capital of California is _____Sacramento_____.

2. Three other important cities are _____,

_____, and _____.

3. The state to the north is _____.

4. The states to the east are _____ and

_____.

5. The country to the south is _____.

6. The _____ is to the west.

 B **Working Together** **In a group, draw a map of your city and state.** Show the capital and three other important cities. Share your map with the class.

CD2·TR16

A Listen and repeat.

1. Miami, Florida: 409,719

2. Atlanta, Georgia: 519,145

3. Las Vegas, Nevada: 552,539

4. Washington, D.C.: 588,292

5. Detroit, Michigan: 916,952

6. San Antonio, Texas: 1,328,984

7. Philadelphia, Pennsylvania: 1,449,634

8. Houston, Texas: 2,208,180

9. Oakland, California: 397,067

10. New York, New York: 8,274,527

CD2·TR17

B Listen and write the population.

> 594,210 = five hundred ninety four thousand, two hundred and ten

1. Seattle, Washington _____594,210_____

2. Phoenix, Arizona _____

3. San José, California _____

4. Boston, Massachusetts _____

5. Chicago, Illinois _____

6. Honolulu, Hawaii _____

7. Dallas, Texas _____

8. Greensboro, North Carolina _____

C Pronunciation: Large Numbers Work with a partner. Follow the directions.

Student 1: Read world population numbers 1–4 to Student 2.

Student 2: Cover the page with a piece of paper. Listen to Student 1. Write the numbers. Now, change and read the population numbers 5–8 to Student 1.

Student 1: Cover the page. Listen and write the numbers.

1. Seoul, Korea: 10,421,780

2. Tokyo, Japan: 8,731,000

3. Shanghai, China: 13,481,600

4. Cairo, Egypt: 6,758,581

5. Mexico City, Mexico: 8,836,045

6. Moscow, Russia: 10,452,000

7. Bogotá, Colombia: 7,155,052

8. Mumbai, India: 13,922,000

7

Downtown

Stores and Other Places Downtown

Dictionary

  A **Listen and repeat.**

CD2·TR18

Stores

1. a bank

2. a bakery

3. a bookstore

4. a coffee shop

5. a laundromat

6. a shoe store

7. a supermarket

8. a drugstore

Places Downtown

9. City Hall

10. a library

11. a police station

12. a park

13. a post office

14. a hospital

15. a parking lot

Word Builder

A **Complete.**

1. I mail letters at the _____ *post office* _____.

2. I borrow books at the _____.

3. I buy food at the _____.

4. I buy books at the _____.

5. I wash my clothes at the _____.

6. I deposit money at the _____.

7. I fill my prescriptions at the _____.

8. I walk in the _____.

9. I buy sneakers at the _____.

B **Working Together** **Work in a group.** Write the name of a store or location in your community.

1. park: _____

2. hospital: _____

3. supermarket: _____

4. drugstore: _____

5. bakery: _____

6. coffee shop: _____

7. bank: _____

8. bookstore: _____

9. music store: _____

10. movie theater: _____

11. shoe store: _____

WORD PARTNERSHIPS		
take out		
check out	a book a DVD	from the library
borrow		

Prepositions of Location

  A Listen and repeat.

CD2·TR19

1. The bank is **on the corner of** First Street and Main Street.

2. Mr. Garcia is **in front of** the bank.

3. Mr. Garcia is **in back of / behind** the bank.

4. Mr. Garcia is **next to** the bank.

5. Mr. Garcia is **across from** the bank.

6. Mr. Garcia is **between** the bank and the coffee shop.

  B Listen and complete the map.

CD2·TR20

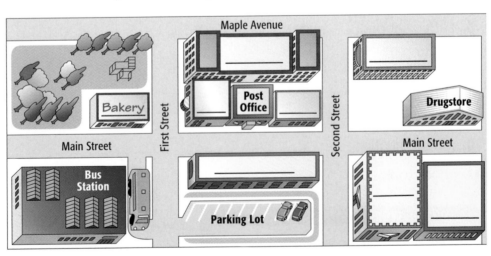

| ~~bakery~~ | shoe store | library | coffee shop |
| supermarket | bookstore | bank | laundromat |

A **Working Together** Give the location of the places on the map.

> The bookstore is next to the bakery.

> The parking lot is behind the school.

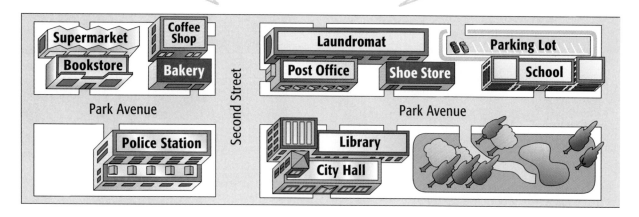

B **Look at the map and write the locations of five buildings.**

1. The supermarket is in back of the bookstore.

2. _____

3. _____

4. _____

5. _____

6. _____

 C **Pronunciation: Checking Information** **Listen and repeat the conversations.**

CD2·TR21

1. A: Where's the shoe store?

   B: It's on Park Avenue.

   A: On Park Avenue?

   B: Yes.

2. A: Where's the parking lot?

   B: It's behind the school.

   A: Behind the school?

   B: That's right.

3. A: Where's the park?

   B: It's next to the library.

   A: Next to the library?

   B: Yes.

4. A: Where's the bakery?

   B: It's across from the police station.

   A: Across from the police station?

   B: That's right.

 D **Working Together** **Practice the conversations in Exercise C with a partner.**
Use different buildings and locations.

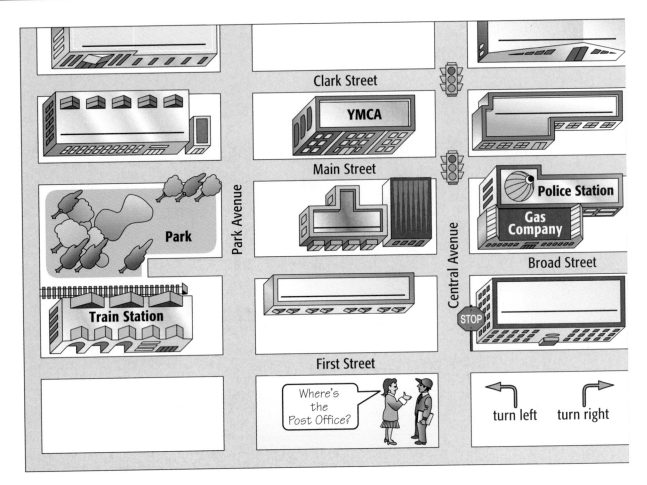

A **Working Together Read the conversations.** Follow the directions and write the locations on the map.

1. A: Where's the library?

    B: Walk three blocks to the first traffic light.

      Turn left.

      The library is two blocks up on your right.

2. A: Where's the art museum?

    B: Walk four blocks to the second traffic light. That's Clark Street.

      Turn left.

      The art museum is about two blocks up on your right.

3. A: Where's the high school?

    B: Walk one block to the first stop sign. That's First Street.

      Turn right.

      The high school is on your left.

traffic light

stop sign

B **Look at the map on page 90.** Read and complete the directions.

traffic light	right	Clark	~~Broad~~
stop sign	left	Main	First

1. A: Where's the gas company?

   B: Walk two blocks to _____Broad_____ Street.

   Turn _____.

   The gas company is on your _____.

2. A: Where's the train station?

   B: Walk one block to the first _____.

   That's _____ Street.

   Turn _____.

   The train station is two blocks up on your _____.

3. A: Where's the park?

   B: Walk two blocks to _____ Street.

   Turn _____.

   The park is about two blocks up, in front of you.

C **Listen and write the locations on the map on page 90.**

CD2·TR22

   1. City Hall   **2.** post office   **3.** hospital   **4.** aquarium

D **Working Together Write the directions to each of the locations.** Then, tell the directions to another student. Can he or she follow your directions?

   1. City Hall   **2.** police station   **3.** aquarium

Walk _____ blocks.

Walk _____ blocks to the first _____.

That's _____ Street.

Turn right.

Turn left.

The _____ is on your right / left.

A Complete these sentences about your local library.

1. The library is on ⸻.

2. The telephone number of the library is ⸻.

3. I **have / don't have** a library card.

4. I can take out ⸻ from the library.

5. I can also borrow ⸻ and ⸻.

B Complete.

Public Library Card Application

⸻ ⸻ ⸻ ⸻/⸻/⸻
Last name   First name   MI   Today's date

☐ Adult ☐ Child   ⸻-⸻-⸻   ⸻
Social Security Number   (If child, signature of parent/guardian)

⸻
Address

⸻ ⸻ ⸻
City   State   Zip Code

Telephone: (⸻) ⸻-⸻

C Complete the sentences.

1. The maps are _____*next to*_____ the dictionaries.

2. The videos are _____ the circulation desk.

3. Edward is standing _____ Theresa at the circulation desk.

4. The periodicals are _____ the bookcase.

5. The newspapers are _____ the circulation desk.

6. The computers are _____ a long table. The table is _____ the circulation desk.

7. Josh is sitting _____ a computer.

8. The children's section is **downstairs / upstairs**.

9. The maps and dictionaries are **downstairs / upstairs**.

D Ask and answer the questions.

1. Where are the librarians?

2. What is Theresa doing?

3. Is she reading a book?

4. Where is Edward?

5. What is he doing?

6. Is he reading a newspaper?

7. Where is Josh?

8. What is he doing?

9. Where is Amy?

10. Is she looking at the periodicals?

11. What is she looking at?

12. Where is Sara going?

E Working Together Go to the library or other place in your school. Write about the location of items or people.

Example: *The periodicals are next to the newspapers.*

1. _____

2. _____

3. _____

4. _____

5. _____

The Big Picture

  A Listen and point to each person in the story.

CD2·TR23

  B Listen and circle.

CD2·TR24

1. **a.** Elena is.   **b.** Jane is.   **c.** Mrs. Lee is.

2. **a.** Michael is.   **b.** Luisa is.   **c.** Michael and Luisa are.

3. **a.** Officer Ortiz is.   **b.** Mr. Thomas is.   **c.** Mark is.

4. **a.** Officer Ortiz is.   **b.** Jane is.   **c.** Mrs. Lee is.

5. **a.** Mark is.   **b.** Joseph is.   **c.** Jane is.

6. **a.** Joseph is.   **b.** Jane is.   **c.** Luisa is.

7. **a.** Joseph is.   **b.** Officer Ortiz is.   **c.** Michael and Luisa are.

8. **a.** Mr. Thomas is.   **b.** Mrs. Lee is.   **c.** Officer Ortiz is.

C (Circle) **and complete.**

1. The playground is _____ *on* _____ Smith Street.
   a. across from   **(b.)** on   **c.** between

2. City Hall is _____ the playground.
   a. across from   **b.** next to   **c.** on the corner of

3. The coffee shop is _____ the bakery.
   a. next to   **b.** between   **c.** behind

4. The parking lot is _____ the laundromat.
   a. across from   **b.** behind   **c.** between

5. Jane and Joseph are sitting _____ the coffee shop.
   a. behind   **b.** in front of   **c.** next to

6. The police station is _____ City Hall.
   a. across from   **b.** behind   **c.** on

7. Officer Ortiz is standing _____ Mrs. Lee's car.
   a. next to   **b.** on   **c.** in front of

D **Write the location of the people in the picture.**

1. Joseph and Jane _____ *are sitting in front of the coffee shop* _____.

2. Michael and Luisa _____.

3. Mr. Thomas _____.

4. Officer Ortiz _____.

5. Elena _____.

E **Complete.**

| watch | read | sit | ~~talk~~ | work | play | get |

1. Mr. Thomas _____ *is talking* _____ to the other driver.

2. Elena _____ the children.

3. The children _____ in the park.

4. Joseph and Jane _____ at tables.

5. Joseph _____ a newspaper.

6. Mark _____ at the coffee shop.

7. Michael and Luisa _____ married.

Read.

My Local Library

Every Saturday morning, my son and I go to the public library. The library is only four blocks from our apartment. We can walk there.

My son and I have library cards. We go to the children's section, and he takes out books and videos about animals. He can borrow books for one month, but he can only borrow a video for three days.

Story Time is at 10:00. He stays downstairs and listens to the librarian read stories. I go upstairs and take a computer class. I don't have a computer at home. I am learning how to use the Internet and how to send e-mail to my family.

At the library, I can use the computer for free. After my class, I stop in the reference section and read a newspaper from my country for a few minutes.

The library is a wonderful place for both me and my son. And best of all, it's free!

B (Circle) *True* or *False*.

1. He drives to the library.	True	(False)
2. His son has a library card.	True	False
3. His son likes books about animals.	True	False
4. They can borrow videos for a month.	True	False
5. He stays with his son at Story Time.	True	False
6. He is learning how to use a computer.	True	False
7. He has a computer at home.	True	False
8. Newspapers are in the reference section.	True	False
9. He likes to read the news from his country.	True	False

Writing Our Stories

A **Read.**

> I am a student at Union County College in Elizabeth, New Jersey. Our school is on West Jersey Street. West Jersey Street is a busy street. The traffic is heavy and noisy all day. There are many stores and buildings on West Jersey Street. Our school is between a small parking lot and the gas company. There is a large clothing store across the street. Our school is convenient to transportation. The train station is across the street, and the bus stop is on the corner. We have one problem. Because our school is in a city, it is difficult to find a parking space.

B **Working Together** **Work in a group.** Draw and label a map of the area around your school. Talk about the locations of different places.

C **Write about the location of your school.** Use your map.

I am a student at _____ in _____ .

Our school is on _____

_____

_____

D **Sharing Our Stories** **Work with a partner and compare your paragraphs.** Which stores or buildings did you both write about?

> **WRITING NOTE**
> Check the prepositions in your story.
> <u>on</u> Market Street
> <u>in</u> San Francisco

A **Discuss.**

1. How do you get directions to somewhere new?

2. Do most people give clear directions?

3. Do you use the Internet to get directions?

B **Read.**

Start.

Go straight.

End.

Take exit.

Turn right.

Get onto Route.

Turn left.

C **Complete the directions.**

START	1. _Start_ at 12 Park Place.	0.0 miles
	2. _____ onto River Road.	2.5 miles
	3. _____ onto Summit Avenue.	0.5 miles
ROUTE	4. _____ Route 68 South.	10.4 miles
EXIT	5. _____ 12.	0.1 miles
	6. _____ on Davis Road.	1.5 miles
	7. _____ onto Morris Avenue.	0.2 miles
END	8. _____ at 52 Morris Avenue.	

Distance: 15.6 miles   Drive time: 35 minutes

D **Look at the directions in Exercise C and answer the questions.**

1. Where is this driver starting?

2. Where is she going?

3. How far is she driving?

4. What is the drive time?

Working Together **Work in a group.** Write directions from your school to a place in your city or state.

Complete the Internet directions form. Write the address of your school and the location from Exercise E.

MAP **DIRECTIONS** NEW INFO

I am starting at: Location

_____

Street Address

_____

City   **State**   **Zip Code**

_____ __ __   _____

I am going to: Location

_____

Street Address

_____

City   **State**   **Zip Code**

_____ __ __   _____

G **Use the Internet to check your directions.**

1. Find a map site on the Internet.

2. Click _Directions_.

3. Fill in the information from Exercise F.

4. Print the directions.

5. Compare your directions from Exercise E and the directions from the map website.

8 Money

  A Listen and repeat.

CD2•TR25

Coins

a penny	a nickel	a dime	a quarter
one cent	five cents	ten cents	twenty-five cents
$.01	$.05	$.10	$.25

CULTURE NOTE

From 1999 to 2009, the United States issued a new series of fifty quarters. Each quarter honors a different state. Do you have any quarters in your pocket? Which state's name is on the back?

Bills

a dollar
$1.00

five dollars
$5.00

ten dollars
$10.00

twenty dollars
$20.00

Word Builder

 A **Listen and repeat.**

CD2·TR26

a. 4¢	$.04	**f.** 50¢	$.50
b. 10¢	$.10	**g.** 62¢	$.62
c. 25¢	$.25	**h.** 75¢	$.75
d. 30¢	$.30	**i.** 85¢	$.85
e. 35¢	$.35	**j.** 99¢	$.99

There are three ways to write cents:

ten cents
10¢
$.10

B **Write the amount.**

a.

_____

b.

_____

c.

_____

d.

_____

e.

_____

 C **Working Together** **Work in a group.** Take out your change and count it together. Write the amount. Who has the most change?

 D **Listen and write the amount.**

CD2·TR27

a. $.02 _____   **d.** _____   **g.** _____

b. _____   **e.** _____   **h.** _____

c. _____   **f.** _____   **i.** _____

WORD PARTNERSHIPS	
	credit card
pay by	check
	cash

Money · **101**

Word Builder

Dollars and Cents

$ 2.50   = two dollars and fifty cents = two fifty
$10.99 = ten dollars and ninety-nine cents = ten ninety-nine
$498.79 = four hundred and ninety-eight dollars and seventy-nine cents
         = four ninety-eight seventy-nine

CULTURE NOTE

The dollar is the monetary unit of the United States. What is the monetary unit in your country?

  A Listen and repeat.

CD2·TR28

a. $1.00   **d.** $4.99   **g.** $127.98

b. $1.50   **e.** $17.49   **h.** $249.99

c. $2.75   **f.** $59.50   **i.** $629.77

  B Listen and write the amount.

CD2·TR29

a. $ 1.00   **d.** _____   **g.** _____

b. _____   **e.** _____   **h.** _____

c. _____   **f.** _____   **i.** _____

  C Pronunciation: Numbers Listen and repeat the numbers.

CD2·TR30

13	14	15	16	17	18	19
30	40	50	60	70	80	90

  D Circle the number you hear.

CD2·TR31

a. (13)   30   **f.** $18 $80   **k.** $14.40 $14.14

b. 14   40   **g.** $19 $90   **l.** $17.20 $70.20

c. 15   50   **h.** $13 $30   **m.** $16.16 $60.16

d. 16   60   **i.** $15 $50   **n.** $18.75 $80.75

e. 17   70   **j.** $19 $90   **o.** $10.50 $10.15

Stores and Prices

A **Working Together** **Talk about the places you like to shop.**

1. I shop at _____ for clothes.

2. I shop at _____ for food.

3. I shop at _____ for toys.

4. I shop at _____ for shoes.

5. I shop at _____ for school supplies.

6. I shop at _____ for electronic equipment.

7. I stop at _____ for gas.

8. I stop at _____ for a cup of coffee.

9. I stop at _____ for the newspaper.

10. _____ is a convenience store in my area.

B **Working Together** **Complete the sentences with a price.**

1. A first-class stamp is _____.

2. The local newspaper is _____.

3. A cup of coffee is _____.

4. A gallon of regular gas is _____.

5. A bottle of water is _____.

6. A DVD is _____.

7. A video rental is _____.

8. A movie ticket is _____.

9. A round-trip plane ticket to my country is _____.

10. A laptop computer is about _____.

C **Working Together** **Bring in sales circulars.** Discuss.

1. Where is the sale? When is the sale?

2. List four items on sale. What is the regular price? What is the sale price?

| **How much is** a map? | **It's** $9.00. |
| **How much are** the markers? | **They're** $3.50. |

A Write the names of items you can buy at an office supply store.

1. _____
2. _____
3. _____
4. _____
5. _____
6. _____
7. _____
8. _____
9. _____

B Ask and answer questions about the price of each item.

$9.00

1. a map

99¢

3. a ruler

$24.95

5. a shredder

How much is this map?

It's $9.00.

$5.99

2. a stapler

$16.50

4. a calculator

$99.00

6. a printer

C Ask and answer questions about the price of each item.

1. batteries

3. crayons

5. envelopes

How much are the batteries?

They're $5.39.

2. scissors

4. markers

6. paper clips

D Complete the questions and answers.

1. How much ___is___ this stapler?   ___It's___ $5.99.

2. How much _____ the calculator?   _____ $16.50.

3. How much _____ the batteries?   _____ $5.39.

4. How much _____ the envelopes?   _____ $1.29.

5. How much _____ a ruler?   _____ 99¢.

6. How much _____ a shredder?   _____ $24.95.

7. How much _____ the paper clips?   _____ 59¢.

E **Working Together** Work with a partner and figure out your change.

1. Buy a box of paper clips for 59¢. Give the cashier $1.00.

2. Buy a pair of scissors for $3.99. Give the cashier $5.

3. Buy a stapler for $5.99. Give the cashier $10.

4. Buy a shredder for $24.95. Give the cashier $30.

5. Buy a map for $9.00 and a pack of batteries for $5.39. Give the cashier $20.

A **Check (✔) the machines that you use .**

_____ copy machine   _____ vending machine

_____ gas pump   _____ parking lot meter

_____ self-checkout machine _____ washer / dryer

> For instructions, use the simple form of the verb.
>
> **Insert** your cash.
> **Push** the button.
> **Take** your change.

B **Working Together** **Practice giving directions.** Act out the directions.

cover coin slot tray

Directions

1. Open the cover.

2. Place your document on the glass, face down.

3. Close the cover.

4. Insert your money in the coin slot.

5. Press "Copy."

6. Take your copy from the side of the copy machine.

7. Open the cover and take your original.

C **Complete the directions for using a vending machine.**

take   ~~choose~~   take   insert   press

1. _____Choose_____ the item you want.

2. _____ the correct numbers.

3. _____ the money.

4. _____ your item.

5. _____ your change.

D **Put the directions for using an ATM machine in order.**

_____ Select *Withdraw Cash*.

_____ Take your cash.

___1___ Insert your ATM card.

_____ Take your receipt.

_____ Put in your PIN number.

_____ Don't forget to take your ATM card!

_____ Choose the amount you want.

E **Write the directions for using an ATM machine.**

First, insert your ATM card. Next,

_____

_____

_____

_____

Words to give order to directions
First,
Next,
Then,
Finally,

 F **Working Together** **Talk about how to use the self-checkout in a store.** Write the steps.

 A **Listen to the conversation.** Complete the sentences.

CD2·TR32

1. Katrina can't study because _____*it's too noisy*_____.

2. She is going to study in the _____.

3. Katrina and Fabio are going to go to the _____.

4. She is going to buy a _____, a _____, and a _____.

5. She also needs _____.

6. Fabio is going to look at a _____.

CD2·TR33 **B** **Listen to the conversation.** Then, write the items that Katrina and Fabio buy. Write the prices.

1. _____a desk_____ _____$119_____

2. _____ _____

3. _____ _____

4. _____ _____

5. _____ _____

C **Write the total amount for all the items.**

_____

CD2·TR34 **D** **Listen and write the responses.**

1. A: This desk is nice. **B:** _____It's too big_____ .

2. A: How about this desk? **B:** _____ .

3. A: This one is the right size. **B:** _____ .

4. A: Do you like this chair? **B:** _____ .

5. A: How about this one? **B:** _____ .

6. A: How about this one? **B:** _____ .

7. A: How much is the lamp? **B:** _____ .

A **Read.**

I like houseware stores. There is a beautiful houseware store in the mall near my house. It sells kitchen, bedroom, and bathroom items. My favorite department is the kitchen department. I buy something there every month, such as glasses or a new pot. The store sends ads and catalogs to my home. Every month, the store gives me a coupon for 20 percent off any item.

Mimi

There is a bookstore in my city that is as big as a supermarket. It has a small café. People order tea or coffee and look at books. The store has every kind of book. I speak Spanish, and it has a section with many books in Spanish. I can buy Spanish newspapers and magazines, too. I love cookbooks. Every month, I buy a new cookbook. I have a special credit card for that store, and I get 30 percent off every book I buy.

Carla

B **Check (✔).**

	Mimi	Carla
1. She has a credit card for her favorite store.		✔
2. She receives store coupons.		
3. She gets a 30 percent discount on the things she buys.		
4. She checks store ads.		
5. She buys something at her favorite store every month.		
6. She receives catalogs from the store.		
7. She gets 20 percent off one item every month.		

C **Talk about your favorite stores.**

1. What is your favorite store?

2. Where is it?

3. Is it large or small?

4. How often do you shop there?

5. Do you have a credit card for the store?

6. Do you look for sales?

A **Read.**

> My favorite store is an electronics store. There is an electronics store on the highway near my house. It sells TVs, computers, printers, cameras, telephones, and other equipment. I go there almost every week. I have a laptop computer and a digital camera. I like to take pictures of my family and friends. I want a photo printer. It's about $99. When there is a sale, I'm going to buy one.

B **Complete the information.** Then, write about your favorite store.

1. My favorite store is _____.

2. It is **near / far from** my home.

3. It sells _____, _____, and

_____.

4. I go there _____.

C **Sharing Our Stories** **Read your story to a partner.** Complete these sentences.

1. My partner's favorite store is _____.

2. My partner likes to buy _____.

3. I **never / sometimes / often** go to my partner's favorite store.

> **WRITING NOTE**
> **Use capital letters for the name of a store:**
>
> <u>B</u>est <u>E</u>lectronics
> <u>S</u>weet <u>T</u>hings <u>B</u>akery

```
ELECTRONICS
CITY
137 Route 68
                date: 11/15
Photo Printer              $59.00
Photo Paper                  9.00
Ink #445                    18.98

Subtotal                    86.98
Sales Tax 7%                 6.09

              TOTAL DUE    $93.07
CREDIT CARD                $93.07
xxxx-xxxx-xxxx-1234
```

A **Look at the store receipt and complete the sentences.**

1. The name of the store is _____ Electronics City _____.

2. The date of the sale was _____.

3. This person bought _____ items.

4. The photo printer was $ _____.

5. The photo paper was $ _____.

6. The cost of all three items was $ _____.

7. In this state, the sales tax is _____%.

8. The sales tax for these items was $ _____.

9. The total for everything was $ _____.

10. This person paid by _____.

Keep your receipt

1. You can use receipts to check your credit card statement.
2. You might need the receipt to return an item.

 A In a small group, answer these questions.

1. What is the name of this store?

2. When is the sale?

3. What time is the store open?

4. How much will you save on the laptop computer?

5. What is the original price of the TV? How much is the sale price? What size is the TV?

6. How much is the digital camera?

7. Are cell phones on sale?

8. Is this a good sale?

Unit 9 Transportation

A Busy Street

  A Listen and repeat.

CD2·TR35

1. a car
2. a driver
3. a bus stop
4. a bus
5. passengers

6. a taxi
7. a bicycle
8. a helmet
9. a truck
10. an airplane

11. a street
12. a sidewalk
13. a traffic light
14. a shopping bag
15. a briefcase

WORD PARTNERSHIPS	
get on	a bus
get off	a train
get into	a car
get out of	a taxi

Word Builder

A Complete.

1. The boy on the bicycle is wearing a red _____helmet_____.

2. Two people are crossing the street. The _____ is red.

3. Two _____ are getting on the bus.

4. The man with the briefcase is walking on the _____.

5. A woman is getting on the bus. She's carrying a _____.

B Working Together Complete the sentences with a partner. You can use the same name more than once.

1. _____Elena_____ is getting into the taxi.

2. _____ is carrying a briefcase.

3. _____ and _____ are crossing the street.

4. _____ is riding a bicycle.

5. _____ and _____ are getting on the bus.

6. _____ is running for the bus.

7. _____ is wearing a helmet.

8. _____ is carrying a shopping bag.

9. _____ is getting out of the taxi.

10. _____ is wearing a backpack.

C Working Together Complete. Then talk about your answers.

1. I live _____ miles/km from school.

2. I **drive / don't drive**.

3. I **walk / drive / take the bus / take the train / take the subway** to school.

4. I live _____ miles/km from work.

5. I **walk / drive / take the bus / take the train / take the subway** to work.

6. The **bus / train / subway** is $ _____.

7. A gallon of gas is $ _____.

A **Working Together** **Answer these questions with a partner.** Do not look back at the picture on page 114.

> I **am studying** English.
>
> The teacher **is looking** at her book.
>
> The students **are talking**.

1. Who is running for the bus?

2. How many people are getting on the bus?

3. What is Ivan carrying?

4. Is Ivan talking on his cell phone?

5. Is the woman getting into the taxi?

6. How many people are crossing the street?

7. Is the boy on the bike wearing a helmet?

  B **Look at the picture on page 114.** Talk about what the people are doing.

> Ahmed and Briana are getting on the bus.

1. get on the bus

2. get out of the taxi

3. run for the bus

4. walk along the sidewalk

5. cross the street

6. carry a shopping bag

7. get into the taxi

8. carry a briefcase

9. ride his bicycle

 C **Working Together** **Work with a group.** Look around your class. In your notebooks, write five sentences about what students are doing now.

> Carlos is sharpening his pencil. Maya is walking into the classroom. She's late today.

D **Answer the questions.**

Picture 1

Picture 2

Picture 1

1. Where are these people?

_____

2. How many people are waiting for the bus?

_____

3. What are the men carrying?

_____

4. What is the woman on the right doing?

_____

Picture 2

1. Where is the man?

_____

2. What is he doing?

_____

3. What is he looking at?

_____

4. What is he holding?

_____

Questions	Affirmative Answer	Negative Answer
Are you **driving?**	Yes, I **am.**	No, **I'm not.**
Is he **walking** to work?	Yes, he **is.**	No, he **isn't.**
Are they **taking** the bus?	Yes, they **are.**	No, they **aren't.**

A **Answer the questions.**

1. Are you sitting in class now? _____

2. Are you studying English? _____

3. Are you talking with a partner now? _____

4. Are you writing in your book? _____

5. Is your teacher sitting? _____

6. Is your teacher writing on the board? _____

7. Is your teacher wearing a sweater today? _____

8. Are the students taking a test now? _____

9. Are the students looking at their books? _____

 B **Working Together** **Ask and answer the questions about the picture on page 114.**

1. Are Ahmed and Briana getting on the bus?

2. Is Ahmed carrying a briefcase?

3. Is Carrie running for the bus?

4. Is David getting into the taxi?

5. Is Elena driving the taxi?

6. Are Frank and Joni crossing the street?

7. Are Frank and Joni talking?

8. Is Harry riding his bicycle to school?

9. Is Ivan crossing the street?

10. Is Ivan going to work?

Write questions and answers about the picture.

1. Is he talking on the phone?   Yes, he is.

talk on the phone

2. _____   _____

wear a headset

3. _____   _____

use his GPS

4. _____   _____

wear sunglasses

5. _____   _____

snow

6. _____   _____

drink a cup of coffee

7. _____   _____

wear his seat belt

 Working Together Draw a picture of a person performing an action. The other students will guess what the person is doing.

> Is he washing the dishes?

> No, he isn't.

> Is he doing the laundry?

> Yes, he is.

Where	**am**	I	**going?**	I'm going to the bank.
What	**are**	you	**doing?**	I'm reading.
Where	**is**	he	**standing?**	He's standing at the bus stop.
What	**are**	they	**carrying?**	They are carrying their books.

CD2·TR36

A **Listen to each question.** Write the name of the correct person.

1. _____Tomi_____   4. _____   7. _____

2. _____   5. _____   8. _____

3. _____   6. _____   9. _____

B **Working Together** **Ask and answer** *wh-* **questions about the picture.**

> What is Roberto doing?

> He's talking on the phone.

C Complete the questions with *Who, Where, What, Why.*

1. _____Where_____ is everyone standing?   At the bus stop.

2. _____ is Roberto talking to?   His boss.

3. _____ is Jade standing?   Next to Roberto.

4. _____ is Lynda doing?   She's reading.

5. _____ is Sophia standing?   Next to her mother.

6. _____ is Tomi looking at?   A bus schedule.

7. _____ is Greg running?   Because the bus is coming.

D Write questions and answers about the picture.

1. Where / Roberto / stand?   Where is Roberto standing?

   He's standing at the bus stop.

2. What / Jade / carry?   _____

   _____

3. What / Lynda / do?   _____

   _____

4. Who / Chandi / talk to?   _____

   _____

5. Where / Mehmet / sit?   _____

   _____

E Working Together Bring in interesting pictures from newspapers. Write three questions about the picture. Ask another group to answer the questions.

1. _____

2. _____

3. _____

A **Circle** the things that people are carrying or holding.

> (a ticket)   a pocketbook   an umbrella   a briefcase
>
> a cup of coffee   a cell phone   money   a newspaper
>
> a computer   a camera   a backpack   a shopping bag

B **Listen and write each *Who* question.** Then, write the answer.

CD2·TR37

1. Who is running for the train?   Jason is.
2. _____   _____
3. _____   _____
4. _____   _____
5. _____   _____
6. _____   _____
7. _____   _____

C Listen to each sentence. Who is talking?

CD2·TR38

1. ____Alissa____ is talking to ____Kalee____.

2. _____ is talking to _____.

3. _____ is talking to _____.

4. _____ is talking to _____.

5. _____ is talking to _____.

D Ask and answer *yes/no* questions about the picture.

> Is Lee looking at the train?

> No, he isn't.

1. Lee / look at / the train?

2. Kalee and Alissa / drink coffee?

3. Kalee and Alissa / sit on the bench?

4. the conductor / stand on the train?

5. Fabio / talk to the conductor?

6. Paul / listen to music?

7. Emily / get on the train?

8. Paul and Kelly / talk to each other?

9. Kelly / read the newspaper?

10. Jason / run for the train?

E Listen to the story and complete the questions.

CD2·TR39

1. Where ____is Emily standing____? Next to the train.

2. What _____? She's crying.

3. Why _____? Because Tom is leaving.

4. Where _____? He's going to New York.

5. What _____? "Don't cry."

Reading

A **Discuss. Then read.**

1. Do you own a bicycle? Do you ride it to school or to work?

2. What is a bike path? Are there bike paths in your city?

Travel by bicycle is healthy. It is cheap, it saves gas, and it is good for the environment. What are the most bike-friendly cities in the world?

Amsterdam, Netherlands, is the bike capital of the world. Forty percent of the people ride a bicycle to work. Amsterdam is building a parking garage for 10,000 bicycles at the train station.

In Bogotá, Colombia, people enjoy *Ciclovía*. On Sundays, people cannot ride their cars on many city streets. More than a million people bike, walk, run, and exercise on the city streets.

In the United States, Portland, Oregon, has more than 65 miles (100 km) of bike paths. These are small roads only for bicycles. It is easy to travel by bike. At school, children learn about bicycle safety. If you do not have enough money to buy a bicycle, the city will give you a bike, a helmet, and a lock.

B **Circle a good title for this story.**

1. Bicycles and Health   2. Biking in Amsterdam   3. Bike-Friendly Cities

C **Write the name of the city or cities.**

1. City streets are closed on Sundays. _____

2. This city teaches children about bicycle safety. _____

3. This city gives free bicycles to people. _____

4. Forty percent of the people bike to work. _____

5. There are many bike paths in this city. _____

6. This city has a parking garage for bicycles. _____

A Read.

> I live in Portland, Oregon. I don't have a car.
> A car is expensive, gas is expensive, and insurance
> is expensive.
>   I go to school, and I work. I live close to school,
> so I walk to school. I live six miles from work. When
> the weather is clear, I ride my bike to work. It is easy
> and safe. It only takes me 30 minutes. My company
> has a place to park bicycles. It rains a lot in the winter.
> When it rains, I take the bus to work.
>   One problem is food shopping. I go to the supermarket
> once a week, and I have four or five bags of food. I call
> a taxi to take me home.

B Complete the sentences.

1. I live in _____.

2. I **do / don't** have a car.

3. I live _____ miles/km from school.

4. I _____ to school.

5. I live _____ miles/km from work.

6. I _____ to work.

C Write about your daily transportation.

D Sharing Our Stories Read your partner's story and discuss.

1. Who lives closer to school?

2. Who walks to work or to school?

3. What problem does your partner have with
   transportation?

WRITING NOTE

Before you hand your paper to
your teacher, check the spelling.
If you write on a computer, use
the "Spell Check" function.

English in Action

 A **Read and practice the conversations.**

BUS STOP

BUS SCHEDULE	
BEACH	M2
CLINTON	M7
DAVIS MALL	M12
PATERSON	M15
TRAIN STATION	M19

1. A: I'm going to Clinton.
Which bus do I take?

   B: You want the M7.

2. A: Is this the bus to the mall?

   B: No, you want the M12.

3. A: Is this the bus to Paterson?

   B: Yes.

   A: When is the next bus?

   B: In about ten minutes.

 B **Working Together** **You are at the bus stop.** Write a conversation. Act it out.

A: _____

B: _____

A: _____

B: _____

C Look at the bus schedule and complete the information.

Bus 12 Newton to Bayside	Broad St. & 2nd Street	Broad Street & 25th Street	Davis Mall	Canal Street & Pine Ave.	Bayside Hospital
	7:00	7:11	7:19	7:25	7:40
	7:30	7:41	7:49	7:55	8:08
	8:00	8:11	8:19	8:25	8:40
	8:30	8:41	8:49	8:55	9:08
	9:00	9:11	9:19	9:25	9:40
	10:00	10:11	10:19	10:25	10:48
	11:00	11:11	11:19	11:25	11:48
	12:00	12:11	12:19	12:25	12:48
	1:00	1:11	1:19	1:25	1:48
	2:00	2:11	2:19	2:25	2:48
	3:00	3:11	3:19	3:25	3:48
	3:34	3:45	3:53	3:59	4:12
	5:15	5:26	5:36	5:42	5:55
	5:30	5:41	5:51	5:57	6:10
	6:00	6:11	6:19	6:25	6:40
	7:00	7:11	7:19	7:25	7:40
	9:00	9:11	9:19	9:25	9:40

1. The first bus at Broad Street and 2ⁿᵈ Street is at _____.

2. The 7:00 A.M. bus from Broad Street and 2ⁿᵈ Street arrives at Bayside Hospital at _____.

3. It takes _____ minutes to go from Broad Street and 2ⁿᵈ Street to the Davis Mall.

4. It's 7:20 A.M. You are at Broad and 2ⁿᵈ Street. The next bus is at _____.

5. It's 9:00 A.M. You are at the Davis Mall. The next bus is at _____.

6. Brian lives in Newton near 2ⁿᵈ Street and he works at the Davis Mall. Work begins at 9:00 A.M. He gets the bus at _____.

7. Nellie lives near Canal Street. Her mother is in Bayside Hospital. She wants to visit her at 4:00 P.M. She is going to take the bus at _____.

8. The last bus from the Davis Mall is at _____.

 D Working Together With a partner, write two sentences about the bus schedule. Use the same format as Exercise C. One piece of information is missing. Then, ask another group to complete your sentences.

Dictionary

Clothing and Colors

CD2·TR40

 A **Listen and repeat.**

Clothing

1. a shirt

2. pants

3. jeans

4. shorts

5. a jacket

6. a belt

7. a suit

8. a sweater

9. a dress

10. a skirt

11. a blouse

12. underpants

13. a bra

14. a tie

15. briefs

16. a T-shirt

17. socks

18. a bathing suit

19. sneakers

20. sandals

21. shoes

22. boots

23. a coat

24. a hat

25. a cap

26. gloves

Colors

1. a red cap

2. an orange cap

3. a blue cap

4. a white cap

5. a green cap

6. a black cap

7. a purple cap

8. a brown cap

9. a yellow cap

10. a beige cap

Sizes

1. extra small (XS)

2. small (S)

3. medium (M)

4. large (L)

5. extra large (XL)

WORD PARTNERSHIPS		
try on		pants
put on	a pair of	shoes
		socks
take off		gloves

Word Builder

A Complete.

Clothes for hot weather

shorts _____

_____ _____

_____ _____

Clothes for cold weather

_____ _____

_____ _____

_____ _____

B Cross out the word that doesn't belong.

1. pants, jeans, shorts, ~~T-shirt~~

2. shirt, blouse, T-shirt, sandals

3. sneakers, sandals, hat, shoes

4. coat, hat, gloves, bathing suit

5. blouse, tie, skirt, dress

6. sweater, briefs, underpants, bra

7. jacket, sweater, coat, shorts

> Who is wearing glasses?
> Marc is.
> No one is.

 C Look at your classmates. Ask and answer the questions.

1. Who is wearing sneakers?

2. Who is wearing a sweater?

3. Who is wearing a dress?

4. Who is wearing a white shirt?

5. Who is wearing a tie?

6. Who is wearing sandals?

7. Who is wearing black pants?

8. Who is wearing jeans?

 D Discuss.

1. How many pairs of shoes do you have?

2. How many pairs of jeans do you have?

3. What's your favorite color for clothes?

4. What do you usually wear to school?

5. What do you usually wear to work?

6. Do you wear a uniform at work?

7. What are you wearing now?

a uniform

A **What is Amy wearing?**

I'm **wearing** a sweater.
She's **wearing** jeans.
They**'re wearing** hats.

A   B   C

🔊 **B** **Listen.** What is Amy wearing? Write the letter of the correct picture.
CD2·TR41

1. _B_   3. ____   5. ____   7. ____   9. ____

2. ____   4. ____   6. ____   8. ____   10. ____

🔊 **C** **Pronunciation: Stress** **Listen for the stress.** Put an accent mark over the
CD2·TR42   stressed words.

1. Is Amy wearing white pants?   No, she's wearing bláck pants.

2. Is Amy wearing a blue jacket?   No, she's wearing a green jacket.

3. Is Amy wearing a red dress?   No, she's wearing a blue dress.

4. Is Amy wearing a blue belt?   No, she's wearing a white belt.

5. Is Amy wearing brown sandals?   No, she's wearing white sandals.

6. Is Amy wearing black shorts?   No, she's wearing beige shorts.

👥 **D** **Working Together** **Ask and answer the questions about your classmates'**
clothes.

Is Carlos wearing
a green shirt?

No, he's wearing
a <u>blue</u> shirt.

Dictionary

   **A** **Listen and repeat.**

CD2·TR43

Weather

1. It's sunny.

2. It's cloudy.

3. It's windy.

4. It's raining.

5. It's snowing.

6. It's foggy.

7. It's hot.

8. It's warm.

9. It's cool.

10. It's cold.

Seasons

11. spring

12. summer

13. fall

14. winter

CD2·TR44

A **Listen to the weather.** Find the city and write the temperature on the map.

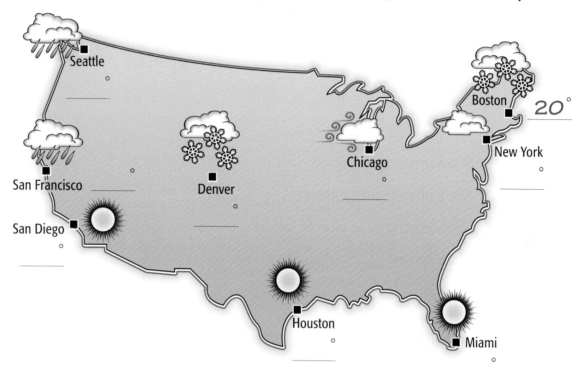

B **Write about the weather in each city.** Use words from the box.

| cold | cloudy | cool | hot | raining | snowing | sunny | warm | windy |

1. It's _____ cold _____ and _____ snowing _____ in Boston.

2. It's _____ and _____ in New York.

3. It's _____ and _____ in Miami.

4. It's _____ and _____ in Houston.

5. It's _____ and _____ in San Diego.

6. It's _____ and _____ in San Francisco.

7. It's _____ in Seattle.

8. It's _____ in Denver.

9. It's _____, _____, and _____ in Chicago.

C **What is the weather in your area today?**

A **Complete the sentences with *a*, *an*, or *X* (for no article).**

a shirt
a pair of shorts
an old belt
jeans

1. He's wearing __*a*__ pair of jeans.

2. He's wearing ____ orange T-shirt.

3. He's wearing ____ sneakers.

4. He's wearing ____ belt.

5. He's wearing ____ briefs.

6. She's buying ____ dress.

7. She's buying ____ gloves.

8. She's buying ____ pair of sandals.

9. She's buying ____ old sweater.

10. She's buying ____ coat.

B **Work with a partner.** Answer the questions.

1. What season is it?
   It's _____.

2. What's the weather?
   It's _____.

3. What is she wearing? _____

   _____.

4. What season is it?
   It's _____.

5. What's the weather?
   It's _____.

6. What is he wearing? _____

   _____.

C **Working Together** **Write a description of a classmate's clothes.** Read the description to the class. The other students will guess the correct student.

  **Josh needs a new pair of shoes.** Listen to the story and number the pictures from 1 to 8.

CD2·TR45

1

  B **Working Together** **Retell the story in your own words.** What is happening in each picture?

Josh is walking into a shoe store.

  C **Working Together** **One student will act out the story of Josh buying a new pair of shoes.** Another student will describe the actions.

> How much **is** this hat?   **It's** $12.00
> How much **are** these socks? **They're** $5.00.

A Complete.

1. How much <u>is</u> <u>this</u> hat?   <u>It's</u> $15.
2. How much <u>are</u> <u>these</u> sandals?   <u>They're</u> $20.
3. How much _____ _____ skirt?   _____ $28.
4. How much _____ _____ gloves?   _____ $17.
5. How much _____ _____ briefs?   _____ $7.
6. How much _____ _____ sweater?   _____ $30.
7. How much _____ _____ tie?   _____ $17.
8. How much _____ _____ shorts?   _____ $22.

B Working Together **Work with a partner.** Put a price on each tag. Then, ask and answer questions about the prices.

| How much is this belt? | $16.00. | How much are these shoes? | They're $37.00. |

The Clothing Store

A Listen and complete the conversation.

CD2·TR46

Clerk: Hello. Can I help you?

Customer: Yes. _____.

Clerk: What size?

Customer: _____.

Clerk: The shirts are here.

Customer: _____. _____?

Clerk: It's $50. But today it's on sale for $25.

Customer: Great. I'll take it.

B Listen and complete the conversation.

CD2·TR47

Clerk: Hello. Can I help you?

Customer: Yes. _____.

Clerk: What size?

Customer: _____.

Clerk: Here they are.

Customer: _____. _____?

Clerk: They're usually $30. But today they're on sale for $19.

Customer: Great. I'll take them.

 C **Working Together** **Write a conversation between a clerk and a customer.** Then, act it out.

CD2·TR48

A **Listen.** (Circle) the clothes that Monica is going to buy.

| (coat) | gloves | sneakers | hat |
| dress | skirt | sweater | socks |

CD2·TR48

B **Listen again and** (circle) *True* or *False*.

1. Monica is in the shoe store.	True	(False)
2. Monica is shopping with her mother.	True	False
3. It's cold now.	True	False
4. Monica likes the coat she is trying on.	True	False
5. Monica is going to spend a lot of money today.	True	False
6. Monica needs winter clothing.	True	False
7. Monica was in the United States last winter.	True	False
8. It's hot all year in Boston.	True	False

C **Complete the sentences.**

Boston	cold	clothing store	May	~~Cuba~~
winter	snow	temperature	summer	hot

1. Monica is from _____Cuba_____.

2. She came to the United States in _____.

3. She lives in _____.

4. In Boston, it is hot in the _____.

5. In Boston, it is cold in the _____.

6. In January, it is going to _____.

7. In Cuba, the weather is _____ all year.

8. Right now, Monica is in a _____.

9. The _____ is 30°.

10. It's very _____ outside now.

D **Listen and complete the conversations.**

CD2•TR49

1. Monica: I don't like this __weather__. It's ____too____ cold.

   Lydia: It's only December. It _____ cold yet. Wait until January!

2. Lydia: Here's a nice coat. _____.

   Monica: I _____ the color. Do they have a _____ or a _____ coat?

3. Monica: Gloves? _____ do I need gloves?

   Lydia: _____ these gloves. Believe me. You need gloves.

4. Monica: How do you like _____?

   Lydia: It doesn't fit you. It's _____.

5. Monica: Do you like _____?

   Lydia: Yes, it looks _____ on you.

E **Working Together** **Write a conversation between Monica and her sister in the clothing store.** Act out your conversations.

Reading

A Discuss.

1. Which clothing catalogs do you receive in the mail?

2. Did you ever order anything from a catalog? Did you like the item?

B Read these ads from a catalog.

C Complete the information.

1. The raincoat is $_____.

2. The raincoat comes in two colors, beige and _____.

3. You **can / can't** wash the coat.

4. The sweater is **cotton / wool**.

5. You can order the sweater in four sizes: _____, _____, _____, and _____.

6. The sweater is $_____.

7. The order number for the jeans is _____.

8. The jeans have _____ pockets.

9. The jeans are $_____.

10. If you want to order something from this catalog, call _____.

Writing Our Stories

A Read.

Spring in Virginia

I live in Virginia. We have four seasons. The summer is long and hot, and the winter is mild. It doesn't snow very often. Right now, it is spring, my favorite season. The days are warm, and the nights are cool. I usually wear jeans and a shirt.

I am from Puerto Rico. The climate is hot and tropical. It is sunny and hot almost every day. The fall is hurricane season, and we sometimes have bad storms with heavy wind and rain. But most of the time, the weather is beautiful.

Virginia

Atlantic Ocean

Puerto Rico

B Complete the sentences.

I live in _____. We have _____ seasons.

My favorite season is _____ because _____.

I am from _____. We have _____ seasons.

The weather is _____.

C Write about the weather in your area. What is your favorite season? Why? How is the weather in your country?

D Sharing Our Stories Read your partner's story and complete the sentences.

1. My partner is from _____.

2. My partner's country has _____ seasons.

3. My partner's favorite season is _____.

4. He **likes / doesn't like** the weather in this country.

> **WRITING NOTE**
>
> The names of states and countries begin with a capital letter.
>
> Example: Virginia

A Discuss the store signs.

No returns without store receipt.

No returns.
Exchanges only.

CD2·TR50

B **Listen.** Then, act out the conversations with a partner.

Conversation 1

Clerk: Can I help you?

Customer: Yes, I want to return this sweater.

Clerk: Do you have the receipt?

Customer: Yes, here it is.

Clerk: Let's see. The sweater was $29.

Customer: With tax, it was $30.45

Clerk: Do you want to exchange the sweater?

Customer: No, I'd like a refund.

Clerk: Okay. No problem.

PATEL'S CLOTHING STORE

Wool Sweater	$29.00
State Sales Tax	$1.45
TOTAL	$30.45

Don't throw away your receipts. Keep your receipts in a small box or an envelope.

Conversation 2

Clerk: Can I help you?

Customer: Yes, I want to return this sweater.

Clerk: Do you have the receipt?

Customer: No, I don't.

Clerk: Sorry. There are no returns without the store receipt.

 C **Working Together** Act out a conversation between a clerk and a customer. The customer wants to return a pair of jeans to the store.

1. Monica is buying a blue coat for $75. Her hat is $15, and her gloves are $20. What is the total?

2. Monica is buying a hat for her sister. It's $17. Monica is giving the clerk $20. How much is her change?

3. Monica is buying a pair of gloves. They are $23. She is giving the clerk $50. How much is her change?

4. Monica likes a blue sweater. It is $60, but it's on sale for 50% off. How much is the sweater?

5. Monica is trying on a red dress. It's $40. All the dresses in the store are 10% off today. How much is the dress?

E **Every item in the store is 50% off today.** Write the new price.

$30.00

$ 15

$65.00

_____

$60.00

_____

$45.00

_____

$80.00

_____

$15.00

_____

Daily Life

Dictionary

Everyday Activities

CD3·TR1

A **Listen and repeat.**

1. get up

2. take a shower

3. get dressed

4. eat breakfast

5. leave the house

6. work

7. go to school

8. get home

9. cook dinner

10. watch TV

11. check e-mail

12. go to bed

Word Builder

A **Look at the dictionary pictures and number the sentences in order.**

_____5_____ **a.** Eric leaves the house at 8:00.

___1___ **b.** Eric gets up at 7:00.

_____3_____ **c.** After he takes a shower, he gets dressed.

_____2_____ **d.** First, he takes a shower.

_____6_____ **e.** Eric walks to work.

_____4_____ **f.** Eric eats breakfast at 7:30.

B **(Circle)** _True_ **or** _False_ **about** _your_ **schedule.**

1.	I get up very early.	True	False
2.	I take a shower in the morning.	True	False
3.	I eat breakfast every day.	True	False
4.	I work full time.	True	False
5.	I eat lunch at home.	True	False
6.	I study for two hours every day.	True	False
7.	I cook dinner.	True	False
8.	I eat dinner with my family.	True	False
9.	I watch TV in the evening.	True	False
10.	I go to bed early.	True	False

WORD PARTNERSHIPS

take	a break
	a shower
	a walk
	a nap

C **Working Together** **What is your routine?** Number the activities below. Then, tell your partner about your day. Use the words _first, then,_ and _after that._

_____ eat breakfast

_____ go to bed

_____ do my homework

_____ eat dinner

_____ take a shower

_____ get up

_____ get dressed

_____ go to work

_____ watch TV

_____ go to school

_____ eat lunch

A **Listen and repeat.**

CD3·TR2

a. two o'clock
2:00

b. two oh-five
2:05

c. two ten
2:10

d. two fifteen
2:15

e. two thirty
2:30

f. two forty
2:40

g. two forty-five
2:45

h. two fifty
2:50

i. two fifty-five
2:55

j. three o'clock
3:00

B **Write the correct time.**

a. <u>six thirty</u>   **b.** _____   **c.** _____   **d.** _____

  C **Listen and show the time on the clocks.**

CD3·TR3

a.     **b.**    **c.**    **d.**

e.    **f.**    **g.**    **h.**

at 6:00	on Monday	in the morning	from 9:00 to 12:00
at noon	on the weekend	in the afternoon	from Monday to Friday
at night		in the evening	

A Complete the sentences with the correct preposition.

1. Henry gets up ___*at*___ 6:00.

2. Laura takes a shower _____ the evening.

3. Clara works _____ 9:00 _____ 5:00.

4. Allan goes to the supermarket _____ Friday.

5. We eat dinner _____ 7:00.

6. I take a break _____ the morning and _____ the afternoon.

7. I watch TV _____ night.

8. The baby takes a nap _____ the afternoon.

9. Edwin plays soccer _____ the weekend.

10. The children eat breakfast _____ 7:00.

11. The school bus comes _____ 7:30.

12. Daisy studies _____ 8:00 _____ 10:00.

B Ask and answer these questions. Use the correct preposition of time.

> What time do you get up?

> I get up at 7 o'clock.

1. What time do you get up?

2. When do you eat breakfast?

3. When do you leave your house?

4. What hours do you work?

5. When do you do your homework?

6. When do you go to the supermarket?

7. When do you do the laundry?

8. When do you watch TV?

9. When do you eat out?

10. What day do you relax?

Active Grammar

A **Circle the correct form of the verb.**

I You We They	work	every day.
He She	works	

1. Eric **get up /(gets up)** at 7:00 in the morning.

2. I **get up / gets up** early.

3. I **eat / eats** breakfast.

4. My parents **eat / eats** breakfast.

5. I **leave / leaves** the house at 8:00.

6. I **go / goes** to school. I **take / takes** the bus.

7. Eric **go / goes** to work. He **drive / drives**.

8. My parents **work / works** full time. I **work / works** part time.

9. I **study / studies** English from 9:00 to 12:00.

10. The students **have / has** a lot of homework.

CD3·TR4

B **Pronunciation: Final *s* Listen and repeat.**

/s/	/z/	/əz/
get–get**s**	drive–drive**s**	watch–watche**s**
work–work**s**	go–goe**s**	wash–washe**s**
take–take**s**	study–studie**s**	
	have–ha**s**	

CD3·TR5

C **Listen.** Which sound do you hear at the end of each verb: /s/, /z/, or /əz/? Listen again and repeat.

1. leaves _____ z _____

2. plays _____

3. relaxes _____

4. writes _____

5. eats _____

6. does _____

7. makes _____

8. watches _____

9. takes _____

10. reads _____

11. lives _____

12. drinks _____

 A **Work with a partner.** Number the pictures from 1 to 10.

B **Work with a partner.** Write a story about Laura's day. Use your imagination!

Laura has a busy day.

_____

_____

_____

_____

_____

_____

_____

_____

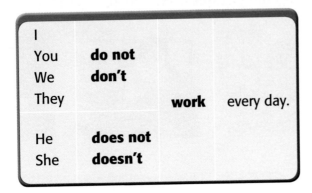

I You We They	**do not** **don't**		
		work	every day.
He She	**does not** **doesn't**		

CD3·TR6

A **Listen to the conversation.** Circle the correct answers about Pierre's day.

1. Pierre **goes** / **doesn't go** to Bayside College.

2. He **has** / **doesn't have** school on Friday.

3. He **goes** / **doesn't go** to school at night.

4. He **has** / **doesn't have** a lot of homework.

5. He **eats** / **doesn't eat** lunch with his friends.

6. He **studies** / **doesn't study** in the library.

7. He **works** / **doesn't work** during the week.

8. He **works** / **doesn't work** in a restaurant.

CD3·TR7

B **Listen to the conversation.** Talk about Maria's day. Some of the sentences are negative.

> She goes to South Street Adult School.

1. she / go / South Street Adult School

2. she / go to school / four days a week

3. she / go to school / in the morning

4. she / have / a lot of homework

5. she / have / time to study

6. she / work

7. she / four children

8. she / be tired at night

No Time to Study

A **Working Together** **Read the conversation between Rosa and her teacher.** Then, act out the conversation with a partner.

Rosa: I'm sorry, Ms. Jackson. I don't have my homework.

Teacher: Again?

Rosa: I don't have time to do my homework.

Teacher: Do you study in the morning?

Rosa: I don't. I have two children. I make breakfast. I drive the kids to school.

Teacher: Do you study during the day?

Rosa: No, I don't. I work full time.

Teacher: Do you study at night?

Rosa: No, I don't. I cook dinner. I take care of the children. And I want to relax.

Teacher: Do you study on the weekend?

Rosa: No, I don't. But that's a good idea.

B **Working Together** **Work with a partner.** Write a conversation between a teacher and a student. Talk about study time.

C **Work with a partner.** Ask these questions. Circle your partner's answers.

1. Do you have a lot of homework?	Yes, I do.	No, I don't.
2. Do you study at the library?	Yes, I do.	No, I don't.
3. Do you study with a partner?	Yes, I do.	No, I don't.
4. Do you speak English with your friends?	Yes, I do.	No, I don't.
5. Do you watch TV in English?	Yes, I do.	No, I don't.
6. Do you study English on the computer?	Yes, I do.	No, I don't.
7. Do you use English at work?	Yes, I do.	No, I don't.
8. Do you read the newspaper in English?	Yes, I do.	No, I don't.

D **Write four sentences about how your partner studies English.**

A **Listen to Emily's day.** Write the correct time under each picture.

CD3·TR8

1. _____

2. _____

3. _____

4. _____

5. _____

6. _____

B **Number the sentences in the correct order.**

_____ She plays baseball after school.

_____ She goes to school.

_____ She takes a shower.

__1__ Emily turns off her alarm clock.

_____ She does her homework.

_____ Then, she watches TV.

_____ After that, she gets up.

_____ She sets her alarm clocks.

_____ Then, she goes to bed.

C Listen again and circle *True* or *False*.

CD3·TR8

1. Emily gets up early. (True) False

2. She takes a shower in the morning. True False

3. Then, she eats breakfast. True False

4. After that, she takes the bus to school. True False

5. Emily likes math. True False

6. Her father watches her play baseball every day. True False

7. She eats dinner with her family. True False

8. She studies for three hours every night. True False

9. At midnight, she goes to bed. True False

D Listen and write each sentence you hear.

CD3·TR9

1. _____

2. _____

3. _____

4. _____

5. _____

6. _____

E Listen to the conversation between Emily and her mother. Complete the sentences.

CD3·TR10

1. Emily is having trouble in _____.

2. Emily studies for _____ hour every night.

3. Emily needs to study for _____ hours every night.

4. She needs to study math from _____ to _____.

Daily Life · **153**

Discuss. Then, read.

1. Do you have a computer?

2. Did you ever study English on the computer?

Nadia

I like studying on the computer. I don't live in an English-speaking country. I don't know anyone who speaks English. On the computer, I study when I want, in the morning or at night. On the computer, I like to use listening sites. I listen to people speak. Sometimes, I listen to the same conversation four or five times. I repeat the sentences. I like using my computer to learn English.

Kim

I have a computer, but I like my class better. For me, class is more interesting. I live in an English-speaking country. I like to speak to other people and use my English. I like to have a teacher. My teacher explains the grammar, and I can ask questions. Also, a class makes me study. I have to come to class, I have to do my homework, and I have to study for tests.

B **Check (✔) the correct answer.**

	Nadia	Kim
1. She has a computer.	✔	✔
2. She lives in an English-speaking country.		
3. She goes to English class.		
4. She can study in the morning or at night.		
5. She has homework.		
6. She has tests.		
7. She likes to listen and repeat.		
8. She likes to study English.		

Writing Our Stories

A Read.

    I am very busy. I don't have much time to study. I go to school on Monday and Wednesday night. I study for one hour on Tuesday and Thursday night.

    I study after my children go to sleep. It's quiet. I study at the kitchen table. I do my homework. Then, I read some of the conversations in the book and I memorize them. Sometimes, I listen to the CD. I repeat or I copy some of the sentences.

    I also try to use my English. I speak English at the store and at the bank. At work, some of the workers speak English, so I talk a little at break time. I am friends with one of the men, and I speak English with him for a few minutes every day.

B Complete. Write or circle words to make sentences about yourself.

1. I study _____ hours a week.

2. I **speak / do not speak** English every day.

3. I like to study **alone / with a partner**.

4. My house is **noisy / quiet**.

5. I study **at home / in the library / in the learning center**.

6. I **use / don't use** a computer to study English.

> **WRITING NOTE**
> Remember to indent each paragraph.

C Write about how you study and practice English.

D Sharing Our Stories Read your partner's story. Complete the information.

1. My partner studies about _____ hours a week.

2. My partner speaks English with _____.

A **How do *you* practice English?** Read each idea. Circle the ones you like.

1. Make flash cards. Study them when you have a few minutes.

2. Watch TV in English. Repeat some of the sentences as you listen.

3. Study from your book. Memorize some sentences.

4. Speak English with co-workers and neighbors.

5. Listen to songs in English. Learn the words.

6. Re-copy compositions and homework. Correct mistakes.

7. Study with another student. Try to speak English!

 B **Working Together** **Work with a group.** Talk about how you study and practice English. Add two more ideas to help you practice your English.

1. _____

2. _____

A   **When can you study?** Complete your typical schedule for the week. Show the time you need for work, meals, and school. Then, schedule your study time.

	Monday	Tuesday	Wednesday	Thursday	Friday	Saturday	Sunday
6:00 A.M.							
7:00							
8:00							
9:00							
10:00							
11:00							
12:00 P.M.							
1:00							
2:00							
3:00							
4:00							
5:00							
6:00							
7:00							
8:00							
9:00							
10:00							
11:00							

B   **Complete.**

1. I am going to study on _____ from _____ to _____.

2. I am going to study on _____ from _____ to _____.

 C   **Working Together Show your schedule to a partner.** Explain when and where you are going to study.

Daily Life • **157**

Food

Dictionary

Snacks, Beverages, and Meals

 A **Listen and repeat.**

CD3·TR11

Breakfast

1. eggs

2. cereal

3. pancakes

4. bacon

5. toast

6. a donut

7. a bagel

Lunch

1. a hamburger

2. French fries

3. a salad

4. soup

5. a turkey sandwich

6. a tuna salad sandwich

7. lettuce

8. a tomato

9. a cucumber

Dinner

1. pasta

2. chicken

3. fish

4. steak

5. rice

6. pizza

7. potatoes

8. green beans

9. corn

10. beans

Beverages

1. coffee

2. tea

3. soda

4. iced tea

5. juice

6. milk

Dessert

1. ice cream

2. cake

3. cookies

4. pie

Fruit

1. bananas

2. apples

3. oranges

4. grapes

5. mangoes

Word Builder

A **Write four foods that you like.** Write four foods that you don't like.

I LIKE . . .

1. _____
2. _____
3. _____
4. _____

I DON'T LIKE . . .

1. _____
2. _____
3. _____
4. _____

CD3·TR12

B **Listen and complete.**

Breakfast

Mike eats breakfast at ___7:15___.

Mike eats _____ and _____.

He drinks _____.

Lunch

Jenny eats lunch from _____ to _____.

Jenny eats _____ with Italian dressing.

She has _____, _____, carrots

and _____ or shrimp on her salad.

She drinks _____.

For dessert, she has _____.

Dinner

Sara and her family eat dinner at _____.

Sara and her family eat _____

or _____.

She likes _____ for dessert.

She and her brother drink _____

or _____.

WORD PARTNERSHIPS	
a slice of	cake
a piece of	pie
two slices of	pizza
three pieces of	toast

CULTURE NOTE

Americans usually eat three meals a day. The big meal is dinner.

C **Working Together** **What food is typical in your country?** Circle and complete. Then, read your answers to a partner.

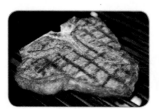   

1. steak   **2.** sushi   **3.** dumplings   **4.** an avocado

1. Steak **is** / **is not** a typical food in _the United States_ .

2. Sushi **is** / **is not** a typical food in _____ .
name of country

3. Dumplings **are** / **are not** a typical food in _____ .
name of country

4. An avocado **is** / **is not** a typical food in _____ .
name of country

D **Make a list of popular foods in your country.** Talk about your list in a group.

Breakfast	Lunch	Dinner
_____	_____	_____
_____	_____	_____
_____	_____	_____

Dessert	Fruit	Beverages
_____	_____	_____
_____	_____	_____
_____	_____	_____

E **Ask and answer the questions with a partner.**

1. What is your favorite food?

2. What is your favorite beverage?

3. What is your favorite dessert?

4. What is your favorite fruit?

A Read.

1. a can of soda **2.** a glass of milk **3.** a cup of coffee **4.** a bottle of juice **5.** a carton of milk **6.** a bowl of soup

B Put the items in the correct columns. You may put an item in more than one column.

~~soda~~	hot chocolate	rice	cereal
chocolate milk	orange juice	water	tea
iced coffee	milk	lemonade	
espresso	coffee	iced tea	

a can of	a bottle of	a cup of
soda		

a glass of	a carton of	a bowl of

> I **like** fruit. | I **don't like** salad.
> He **eats** a banana every morning. | He **doesn't eat** cereal.
> They **eat** meat. | They **don't eat** meat.

A Complete with the correct verb form.

1. I _____cook_____ (cook) dinner every night.

2. My children _____ (like) pizza.

3. My family _____ (eat) dinner together every Sunday.

4. I _____ (like) to cook outside on the grill.

5. Every summer, my neighbor _____ (catch) fresh fish.

6. My mother _____ (shop) at a local supermarket.

7. My children _____ (eat) cereal for breakfast.

8. Mrs. Jones _____ (bake) excellent cakes.

B Listen and complete.

CD3·TR13

> A fussy eater doesn't like many kinds of food.

cheese	tomato
fruit	~~vegetables~~
hamburgers	white bread
peanut butter	milk

1. Christopher doesn't like _____vegetables_____.

2. Christopher doesn't like _____ sauce.

3. He doesn't like _____, either.

4. He doesn't like hot dogs or _____.

5. He doesn't like _____.

6. Christopher likes _____, _____, and _____.

Food · **163**

A Working Together **Work with a partner.** Ask questions and check (✔) the answers.

Do you eat breakfast?

Yes, I do.

Do you like chicken?

No, I don't.

I **don't like** cereal.
We **do not eat** pork.
He **doesn't like** fish.
She **doesn't drink** tea.

do not = don't
does not = doesn't

	Yes	No
1. Do you eat breakfast?		
2. Do you eat pork?		
3. Do you like fish?		
4. Do you like vegetables?		
5. Do you cook at home?		
6. Do you eat with your family?		
7. Do you drink coffee?		

B **Complete the sentences about you and your partner.** Use the information in Exercise A.

1. I _____ (eat) breakfast.

2. My partner _____ (eat) breakfast.

3. My partner _____ (eat) pork.

4. My partner _____ (like) fish.

5. I _____ (like) vegetables.

6. My partner _____ (cook) at home.

7. My partner _____ (eat) with his/her family.

8. I _____ (drink) coffee.

9. My partner _____ (drink) coffee.

> Always = 100%
> Sometimes = 50%
> Never = 0%

> Place adverbs of frequency **before** the main verb.
> I **always** drink water on hot days.
> I **sometimes** drink coffee in the morning.
> I **never** drink coffee at night.

A **Make sentences about you and your family.** Use *always, sometimes,* or *never.* Compare your sentences with a partner's.

1. I _____ eat breakfast.

2. I _____ drink juice at breakfast.

3. I _____ drink coffee in the morning.

4. I _____ eat dinner with my family.

5. I _____ prepare my own meals.

steak on a grill

6. My family _____ eats at fast-food restaurants.

7. My family _____ cooks food outside on a grill.

B **Put the words in the correct order.**

1. always / eats / dinner / my family / together
   My family always eats dinner together.

2. drink / I / at night / coffee / never

   _____

3. my coworker / for lunch / eat / sometimes / and I / salads

   _____

4. desserts / always / my grandmother / delicious / makes

   _____

5. like / fish / or / chicken / for dinner / I

   _____

Working Together **Work with a group.** Discuss the picture.

  Listen and write the orders.

CD3·TR14

Emma: _____

_____

Troy: _____

_____

C **Listen and look at the picture.** Then, read and (circle.)

1. It's Saturday night.		True	(False)
2. Troy and Emma like to sit by the door.		True	False
3. Faye always works on Fridays.		True	False
4. Faye is their favorite waitress.		True	False
5. Emma is having a soda.		True	False
6. Troy and Emma are ordering salads.		True	False
7. Troy is having pasta.		True	False

D **Listen and look at the picture.** Then, read and (circle.)

1. What kind of pizza is the family having?

    a. cheese   **b.** cheese and peppers   **c.** cheese and pepperoni

2. What are the children drinking?

    a. soda   **b.** juice   **c.** milk

3. When do Bob and Ann like to eat out?

    a. On Fridays.   **b.** Every weekend.   **c.** Every night.

4. Why are Bob and Ann eating out tonight?

    a. Because they're hungry.   **b.** Because they're tired.

E **Complete the sentences.**

is ordering	is eating	are drinking	is looking
are sitting	~~are eating~~	is taking	

1. Troy and Emma _____*are eating*_____ at Mario's.

2. They _____ at Faye's table.

3. Emma _____ at the menu.

4. Troy _____ a salad and chicken.

5. Faye _____ Troy's and Emma's orders.

6. Bob's family _____ pizza.

7. They _____ soda.

pepperoni

fish

green pepper

onion

tomatoes

broccoli

mushrooms

pineapple

A **Discuss.** Then, read.

1. Do you like pizza?

2. Where do you eat pizza?

3. What toppings do you like on your pizza?

Clerk: Hello, Buona Pizza. May I take your order?

Customer: Hello, I'd like to order a large pizza.

Clerk: What toppings do you want on it?

Customer: Pepperoni and green peppers.

Clerk: OK. A large pizza with pepperoni and green peppers. That's $8.50. What's your address?

Customer: 1516 Central Avenue.

Clerk: What's your phone number?

Customer: 555-6644.

Clerk: OK. Thank you.

Customer: How long will it take?

Clerk: Thirty minutes. It's Friday, and we're always busy on Fridays.

Customer: OK. Thank you. Good-bye.

Clerk: Thank you for calling Buona Pizza.

B **Answer the questions.**

1. What size pizza did the customer order? _____

2. How many toppings did the customer order? _____

3. What toppings did the customer order? _____

4. It's 7:00. What time will the pizza arrive? _____

A **Read.**

> My favorite holiday is July 4th, Independence Day. My family, my friends, and I always have a barbecue in our backyard. My grandfather cooks the meat. We have steak, chicken, hamburger, and ribs. My mother and my aunts make other food, such as potato salad, green salad, and beans. We drink cold drinks, such as iced tea, soda, or water. For dessert, we always have watermelon and ice cream. Everyone sits in the backyard, and we have a great time.

B **Complete the sentences.**

1. My favorite holiday is _____.

2. On this holiday, we eat **at / in** _____.

3. _____ cooks the meal.

4. We have _____, _____,

   _____, and _____.

5. We drink _____ or _____.

6. For dessert, we have _____.

C **Write about a special holiday and the food you eat on that day.**

WRITING NOTE

Use commas in a list of three or more people, places, or things: cheese, pasta, and meat.

 D **Sharing Our Stories** **Exchange papers with a partner.** Check the commas in your partner's writing.

English in Action

A Read the menu.

The APPLE Diner

PASTA	
Spaghetti with meat sauce	$8.00
Pasta with vegetables	$8.50

MEAT, FISH, and CHICKEN	
Hamburger/Cheeseburger *Special*	$8.99
Chicken and rice	$7.99
7 oz. Steak	$12.99
12 oz. Steak	$15.99
Fish	$14.99

SALADS	
Small green salad	$2.99
Large green salad	$3.99

SOUPS	
Onion Soup	$2.99
Soup of the day	$2.99

BEVERAGES	
Coffee, tea	$1.50
Soda	$1.75
Milk	$1.00

DESSERTS	
Ice cream	$1.99
Apple pie	$2.99

oz. = ounce

B Pronunciation: I'll Listen and write.

CD3·TR16

1. ___I'll have___ a hamburger.

2. _____ the steak.

3. _____ a salad.

4. _____ the pasta.

5. _____ a soda.

6. _____ ice cream.

C Listen and practice the conversation with two classmates.

CD3·TR17

Waiter: Are you ready to order?

Customer 1: Yes, we are.

Waiter: What'll you have?

Customer 1: I'll have onion soup and spaghetti with meat sauce.

Waiter: Anything to drink?

Customer 1: I'll have coffee.

Waiter: And you? What'll you have?

Customer 2: I'll have the cheeseburger special.

Waiter: Would you like a salad?

Customer 2: No, thank you.

Waiter: Anything to drink?

Customer 2: I'll have a soda, please.

D **Complete the conversation.** Then, a few groups of students will act out their conversation for the class.

Waiter:	Are you ready to order?
Customer 1:	Yes, we are.
Waiter:	What'll you have?
Customer 1:	I'll have _____.
Waiter:	Anything to drink?
Customer 1:	I'll have _____.
Waiter:	And you? What'll you have?
Customer 2:	I'll have _____.
Waiter:	Anything to drink?
Customer 2:	I'll have _____.
Waiter:	_____

CULTURE NOTE

In the United States, Americans leave a tip for the waiter or waitress. Waiters and waitresses do not receive large salaries, so tips are important. People usually leave 15%–20% of the check total.

  E **What is the total for each bill?** How much tip will you leave?

HILL'S DINER	
Scrambled Eggs	$3.00
Juice	.75
Coffee	.75
Total	

Mario's Italian Restaurant
2 Salads $8.00
Spaghetti $9.50
Chicken $12.50
2 Coffees $2.50
Total

Jobs

Dictionary

Jobs and Occupations

A Listen and repeat.

CD3·TR18

1. a desk clerk

2. a babysitter

3. a busboy

4. a cashier

5. a cook

6. an electrician

7. a housekeeper

8. a landscaper

9. a laundry worker

10. a manager

11. a plumber

12. a security guard

13. a manicurist

14. a waiter / a waitress

15. a van driver

16. a hair stylist

Word Builder

A **Write the jobs from the dictionary in the correct category.** You can write some jobs in more than one category. Add two more jobs to each category.

Works alone

_____ _____

_____ _____

Works outside

_____ _____

_____ _____

Works in a restaurant

_____ _____

_____ _____

Works in a salon

_____ _____

_____ _____

Works with hotel guests

_____ _____

_____ _____

WORD PARTNERSHIPS		
get	hired	
	fired	
	laid off	
look for		
find	a job	
quit		

B **Match.**

_____g_____ **1.** a van driver

_____ **2.** a desk clerk

_____ **3.** a babysitter

_____ **4.** a waitress

_____ **5.** a cook

_____ **6.** a laundry worker

_____ **7.** a housekeeper

_____ **8.** a manager

_____ **9.** a plumber

_____ **10.** a busboy

a. serves food

b. washes and dries sheets and towels

c. cleans and clears tables

d. takes reservations

e. repairs bathrooms

f. supervises employees

g. drives guests to the airport

h. watches and takes care of children

i. prepares food

j. cleans and vacuums rooms

	Affirmative		Negative
Waiters	**work** in a restaurant.	Cooks	**don't serve** food.
A desk clerk	**works** at the front desk.	A waiter	**doesn't cook** food.

A **Complete.** Use the affirmative form of the correct verb.

color	install
cut	prepare
~~drive~~	wash
fix	wear

1. A van driver _____*drives*_____ guests to the airport.

2. A security guard _____ a uniform.

3. Cooks _____ food for the guests.

4. A manicurist _____ nails.

5. Electricians _____ lights.

6. A hair stylist _____ and styles hair.

7. Laundry workers _____ sheets and towels.

8. A plumber _____ sinks.

B **Complete.** Use the negative form of the correct verb.

~~drive~~	take
make	wash
need	wear
serve	work

1. Managers _____*don't drive*_____ guests to the airport.

2. Babysitters _____ uniforms.

3. A landscaper _____ in an office.

4. A busboy _____ orders from customers.

5. Laundry workers _____ English for their job.

6. Security guards _____ hotel reservations for guests.

7. A desk clerk _____ food.

8. A cashier _____ floors.

Work Schedules

A **Read the schedule.** Complete the information below.

	Sunday	Monday	Tuesday	Wednesday	Thursday	Friday	Saturday
Sam			3-11	3-11	3-11	3-11	3-11
Luis		12-5	12-5			12-5	12-5

1. Sam works ___8___ hours a day.

2. Sam works _____ days a week.

3. Sam works **full time / part time.**

4. Sam doesn't work on _____.

5. Sam starts work at _____.

6. Luis works _____ hours a day.

7. Luis doesn't work on _____.

8. Luis works **full time / part time.**

9. Luis has _____ days off.

10. Luis goes home at _____.

> Full time: 35–40 hours a week
> Part time: under 35 hours a week

 B **Working Together** **Work with a partner.** Complete your work or school schedule. Then, ask about your partner's schedule.

	Sunday	Monday	Tuesday	Wednesday	Thursday	Friday	Saturday
You							
_____							

1. Where do you work?

2. What days do you work?

3. What time do you start work?

4. What time do you finish work?

C **Join two other classmates and answer the questions.**

1. Who works on weekends?

2. Who works at night?

3. Who has a difficult schedule?

4. Who has an easy schedule?

	Questions		Short Answers	
Do	you	work full time?	Yes, I **do.**	No, I **don't.**
	they	wear a uniform?	Yes, they **do.**	No, they **don't.**
Does	he	like the job?	Yes, he **does.**	No, he **doesn't.**
	she	use English at work?	Yes, she **does.**	No, she **doesn't.**

CD3·TR19

A **Listen and complete the questions.** Then, practice the conversation.

A: What do you do?

B: I'm a manicurist in a salon.

A: Do you _____?

B: Yes, I do. I like it very much.

A: Do you _____?

B: I work in the day from 9:00 A.M. to 5:00 P.M.

A: Do you _____?

B: Yes, I do. Many of the hotel guests speak English, and I like to talk to them.

A: _____?

B: No, but I always wear an apron and gloves.

A: _____?

B: Yes, I do. I work full time, so I get good benefits.

A: That's great. _____?

B: Yes, I do. Sometimes I get big tips.

CD3·TR20

B **Pronunciation: *Does he / Does she*** **Listen and repeat.**

1. Does he work full time?   Does she work full time?

2. Does he wear a uniform?   Does she wear a uniform?

3. Does he get benefits?   Does she get benefits?

4. Does he like his job?   Does she like her job?

5. Does he work at night?   Does she work at night?

C **Working Together** **Look at the photos.** Work in a group and write four questions to ask each worker about his / her job. One student will be the waitress. The other students will ask their questions. Repeat for the barber and the desk clerk.

1.	Do you get good tips?
2.	Do you work at night?
3.	
4.	

1.	
2.	
3.	
4.	

1.	
2.	
3.	
4.	

 D **Working Together** **Ask and answer the questions with a partner.**

> Does a cook wear a uniform?

> Yes, he does.

> Do waiters serve food?

> Yes, they do.

CULTURE NOTE

Many companies in the United States pay their employees **benefits** for full time work. Some employees receive benefits for part time work. Benefits include: health and dental insurance, paid vacation, breaks, education, and retirement pension.

1. Does a waitress wear a uniform?

2. Do housekeepers make beds?

3. Does a manager get tips?

4. Do security guards wash towels?

5. Do cashiers give change?

6. Does a manager repair bathrooms?

7. Do plumbers prepare food?

8. Does a waiter serve food?

9. Do landscapers work outside?

10. Does a manicurist cut hair?

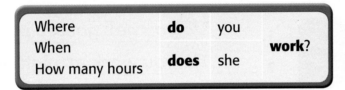

Where	**do**	you	
When			**work**?
How many hours	**does**	she	

 A **Working Together** **Practice the conversation with a partner.** Then, talk about your jobs. When you are finished, talk to three more students.

A: What do you do?

B: I'm a <u>cook</u>.

A: Where do you work?

B: I work at <u>an Italian restaurant</u>.

A: How many hours do you work?

B: I work <u>50 hours a week</u>.

 B **Practice this conversation with a partner.**

A: Where does Marie work?

B: She works at a pharmacy.

A: What does she do?

B: She's a pharmacist.

A: When does she work?

B: She works Fridays, Saturdays, and Sundays.

Name: Marie
Place of Work: Pharmacy
Job: Pharmacist
Days: Friday, Saturday, and Sunday

 C **Working Together** **Talk about the jobs with a classmate.**

1.

Name: Gina
Place of Work:
Office Supply Store
Job: Manager

2.

Name: Paul
Place of Work:
Flower Shop
Job: Florist

3.

Name: David
Place of Work:
Hospital
Job: Custodian

A **Working Together** **Answer the questions about your daily schedule.** Then, sit with a partner and ask the same questions.

Daily Schedule	You	Your Partner
1. What time do you get up?		
2. What time do you eat breakfast?		
3. What time do you leave the house?		
4. What hours do you work?		
5. What time do you study?		
6. What time do you go to bed?		

B **Look at the chart and write six sentences about your partner's schedule.**

My partner gets up at 7:00.

CD3 · TR21
 C **Listen and answer the questions about Luis's job.**

1. What does Luis do?

2. How many hours does Luis work a night?

3. How many cars does he park a night?

4. How many tips does he receive?

5. How many breaks does he have?

CD3 · TR22
 D **Listen and answer the questions about Jane's job.**

1. What does Jane do?

2. How many hours does Jane work a day?

3. How many beds does she change?

4. How many rooms does she clean?

5. How many tips does she get per day?

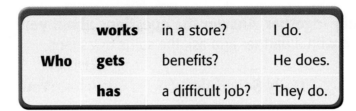

	works	in a store?	I do.
Who	**gets**	benefits?	He does.
	has	a difficult job?	They do.

A **Working Together** **Work with a group of four or five students.** Take turns asking the questions. If a student answers, "I do," write his or her name on the line.

1. Who works in a store? _____

2. Who gets benefits? _____

3. Who works at night? _____

4. Who goes to work early in the morning? _____

5. Who has a difficult job? _____

6. Who has an interesting job? _____

7. Who has a boring job? _____

B **Read and write the question word.** Some words will be used twice.

Do	Does	What	What time	Who	How many

1. __*Does*__ he get benefits?   Yes, he does.

2. _____ hours do you work?   I work 30 hours a week.

3. _____ do you begin work?   I begin work at 7:30 in the morning.

4. _____ works in a restaurant?   A waitress does.

5. _____ do you take a break?   I take a break at 10:30.

6. _____ waiters get tips?   Yes, they do.

7. _____ works outside?   Landscapers do.

8. _____ does Jen do?   She's a hair stylist.

C **Put the words in the correct order to make questions.** Then, write the answers.

No, she works part time.	She works four days a week.
Yes, she does.	~~She's a manicurist.~~
She works from 10:00 to 6:00.	She works at the Sunrise Hotel.

1. does / do / Sheri / what ?

<u>What does Sheri do?</u>   <u>She's a manicurist.</u>

2. work / does / she / where ?

3. does / work / how many days / she

4. full time / does / work / she

5. work / what hours / she / does

6. like / she / does / her job

D **Working Together** **Choose one of the jobs below.** Use your imagination. Write a conversation about the job. Act it out.

1. What do you do?

2. Where do you work?

3. Do you work full time or part time?

4. What's your schedule?

5. Do you like your job?

6. Do you get benefits?

7. When do you have days off?

8. Do you use English at work?

The Big Picture

A **Look at the picture.** Talk about the picture.

1. Where are the employees working?　　**2.** What are their jobs?

B **Listen and** circle.

CD3 · TR23

1. Ricardo is the day manager of the Sunrise Hotel.	True	False
2. The hotel has more than 200 rooms.	True	False
3. The hotel has about 100 employees.	True	False
4. The van driver parks cars.	True	False
5. The hotel has three shifts.	True	False
6. Night employees make more money than day employees.	True	False
7. Everyone works full time.	True	False
8. The salary is high.	True	False
9. Some employees like the hours.	True	False
10. The hotel has job openings.	True	False

Listen and write each question. Then, (circle) the answer.

1. _What does Ricardo Lopez do?_

   a. He's a tourist.　　**b.** He's the night manager.　　**c.** He's the desk clerk.

2. _____

   a. Yes, it does.　　**b.** No, it doesn't.

3. _____

   a. To restaurants　　**b.** To downtown　　**c.** To other hotels

4. _____

   a. The plumber does.　　**b.** The electrician does.　　**c.** Both a and b.

5. _____

   a. Yes, they do.　　**b.** No, they don't.

6. _____

   a. 200　　**b.** 100　　**c.** 20

D **Listen.** Who is the manager speaking to? Complete.

1. He's speaking to the _____housekeeper_____.

2. He's speaking to the _____.

3. He's speaking to the _____.

4. He's speaking to the _____.

5. He's speaking to the _____.

6. He's speaking to the _____.

7. He's speaking to the _____.

E **Answer the questions about the Sunrise Hotel.**

1. What does Ricardo do? _____

2. Who drives guests to the airport? _____

3. Where does the singer work? _____

A Discuss these questions before you read.

1. Do you know anyone who works at a hotel? What do they do?

Richard is a hair stylist at the hotel. He works from Tuesday to Saturday. He works 40 hours a week, from 10:00 A.M. to 6:00 P.M. He is very busy on Fridays and Saturdays because everyone wants to look good for their special parties at the hotel. Most of Richard's customers are tourists or visitors to the city for a special occasion, such as a wedding, an anniversary, or a birthday. He washes, cuts, colors, curls, and blow-dries hair. He enjoys talking with his customers. He stands all day, and he's tired at the end of the day.

Ana is a cook at a hotel. She works from Friday to Sunday. She works 21 hours a week. She starts work at 2:00 P.M. and goes home at 9:00 P.M. She stands all day, so she is tired at 9:00 P.M. She is very busy on weekends because the kitchen has to prepare special meals for parties at the hotel. She cuts vegetables, makes soups, prepares all kinds of meats, and helps with desserts. During the week, Ana goes to cooking school because she wants to become a hotel chef. She wants to manage a hotel kitchen.

B Complete each sentence using *Richard* or *Ana*.

1. _____Richard_____ works full time.

2. _____ works part time.

3. _____ works in the evening.

4. _____ goes to school.

5. _____ works all weekend.

6. _____ stands all day.

7. _____ talks to customers.

A **Read.**

> My Job
>
> I am a security guard. I like my job.
> I work at the Summit Mall in Westbrook.
> I work full time. I work 40 hours a week,
> from Wednesday to Sunday. My hours
> are from 8:30 to 4:30, and I have a half hour for lunch. I
> also have a fifteen-minute break. I receive benefits, too. I have
> medical and dental insurance, vacation, and sick days.
>   My job is easy, but sometimes it is difficult when the mall
> is busy. I walk around the mall all day. I answer questions
> and give directions. I carry a cell phone. In an emergency, I
> call the police or an ambulance.

B **Complete.**

1. I am a _____. **I like / don't like** my job.
                   your job

2. I work at _____ in _____.
                name of the company   location

3. I _____.
        job responsibilities

C **Write about your job.**

> **WRITING NOTE**
>
> The names of companies
> begin with capital letters:
> **C**lothes **C**loset

D **Sharing Our Stories** **Read your partner's story.**
Then, complete the sentences below about your partner's job.

1. My partner is a(n) _____.

2. My partner works at _____.

3. My partner **likes / doesn't like** _____.

English in Action

A **Look at these job ads.** (Circle) the names of the jobs.

Help Wanted
(Bellhop)
Desk Clerk
Western Hotel
137 Kennedy Street
Apply in person.

Job Openings
Housekeepers
Laundry Workers
No Experience.
Will train on job.
Call the Carlton Hotel.
555-6777

Position Available
Cook
Experience Required
Paradise Hotel
Call 644-8899
Ask for Mr. Thomas.

 B **Work with a partner.** Read these classified ads. Ask and answer the questions.

COOK FT 2 years experience required. Excellent pay w/ benefits. Call Thurs. – Sat. 11:00 A.M. – 4:00 P.M. 555-2126

FT = full time

PT = part time

FRONT DESK CLERK for hotel PT Eve shift 3 P.M. – 11 P.M. Will train. Apply in person. Plaza Hotel. Seaside.

LANDSCAPER Immediate FT opening for landscape crew. Valid license required. $9.00/hour. Benefits, vacation. Call today. 555-9328

MAINTENANCE MECHANIC FT Must have painting, plumbing, and electrical skills. Salary based on experience. Good benefits. Sunrise Resort. 555-4334

1. Which jobs are full time?

2. Which job pays $9 an hour?

3. Which jobs have benefits?

4. Which job requires a driver's license?

5. Which jobs require experience?

6. Which job requires painting?

7. Which job has excellent pay?

8. Which jobs do you need to call?

CD3·TR26

C **Listen and read.** Then, practice with a partner.

A: Hello. I'm calling about the job as a security guard.

B: Do you have any experience?

A: Yes. I was a security guard at a bank in Atlantic City for four years.

B: Can you come in for an interview?

A: Yes, I can.

B: We have appointments at 10:00 and at 12:00. What time is good for you?

A: 10:00 is good.

B: Okay. What is your name please?

A: My name is Brian García.

B: Okay, Mr. García. See you at 10:00, and please bring two references.

A: Thank you. See you at 10:00.

CULTURE NOTE

Arrive five to ten minutes early for a job interview.

D **Complete the job application.**

The Sunrise Hotel

Position _____

Name _____
       Last   First   Middle

Address _____
      Number   Street   City   State

Social Security No. _____   Date of birth ____ / ____ / ____

Telephone _____

Work Experience			
From	To	Employer	Position

Signature of applicant _____

14 A Visit to the Doctor

Dictionary

🔊 **A** **Listen and repeat.**

CD3·TR27

Parts of the body

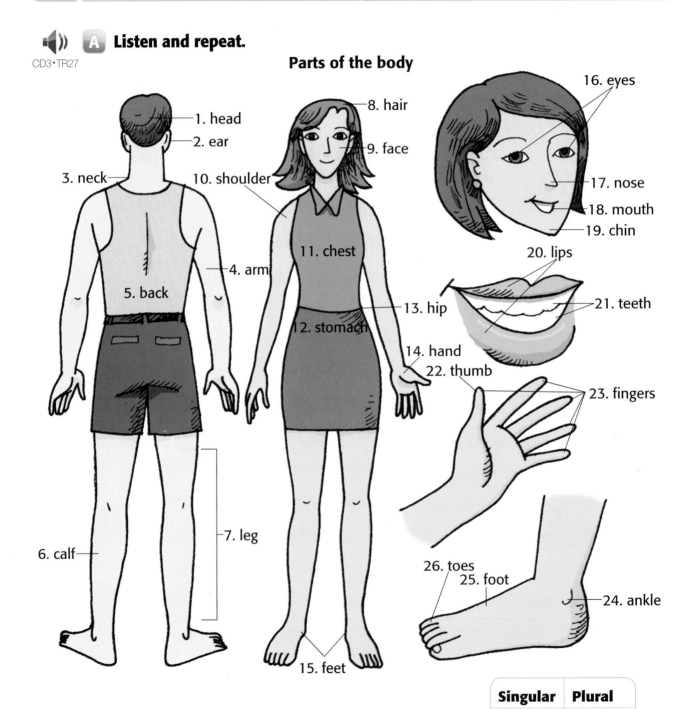

1. head
2. ear
3. neck
4. arm
5. back
6. calf
7. leg
8. hair
9. face
10. shoulder
11. chest
12. stomach
13. hip
14. hand
15. feet
16. eyes
17. nose
18. mouth
19. chin
20. lips
21. teeth
22. thumb
23. fingers
24. ankle
25. foot
26. toes

Singular	Plural
foot	feet
tooth	teeth

B **Listen and repeat.**

CD3·TR28

Health Problems

1. an allergy

2. asthma

3. a burn

4. a cold

5. chicken pox

6. a cough
He's coughing.

7. a fever

8. a headache

9. a sore throat

10. a stomachache

11. a toothache

12. a sneeze
She's sneezing.

  C **Listen and repeat.**

CD3·TR29

Remedies

1. aspirin

2. ibuprofen

3. an ice pack

4. a heating pad

5. an inhaler

6. lotion

7. a dentist

8. a doctor

Word Builder

A **Complete.**

1.

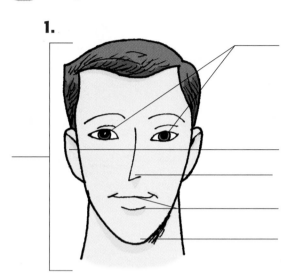

head	chin	eyes
ears	nose	lips

2.

arm	chest
neck	stomach

3.

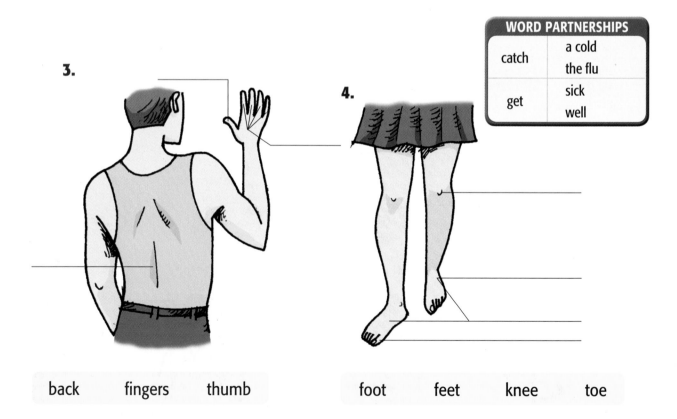

back	fingers	thumb

4.

foot	feet	knee	toe

WORD PARTNERSHIPS	
catch	a cold
	the flu
get	sick
	well

Active Grammar

CD3·TR30

A **Listen.** Look at the pictures and complete.

> My back **hurts**.
> My feet **hurt**.

1. Her ___head hurts___. **2.** Her _____. **3.** Her _____.

4. His _____. **5.** His _____. **6.** His _____.

CD3·TR30

B **Listen again and repeat.**

> hurt = ache

CD3·TR31

C **Pronunciation:** *ache* **Listen and repeat.**

1. a backache **2.** an earache **3.** a headache **4.** a stomachache **5.** a toothache

CD3·TR32

D **Listen and complete the sentences.**

1. He has a _____ *toothache* _____.

2. She has a _____.

3. I have a _____.

4. He has a _____.

5. I have an _____.

E **Working Together** **Act out a problem from page 189 or page 191.** The other students will guess the problem.

I You	**have**	a sore throat.
He She	**has**	

We They	**have**	sore throats.

A **Match.**

_____e_____ **1.** She has the chicken pox.

a.

_____ **2.** She has a sore throat.

b.

_____ **3.** They have allergies.

c.

_____ **4.** They have colds.

d.

_____ **5.** He has a headache.

e.

_____ **6.** They have stomachaches.

f.

_____ **7.** He has asthma.

g.

_____ **8.** She has a fever.

h.

A Listen and repeat.

CD3·TR33

1.

2.

3.

4.

5.

6.

7.

8.

B Read and number the remedies in Exercise A.

_____ Take aspirin.   _____ Drink liquids.   _____ Stay in bed.

_____ Call the doctor.   _____ Put on lotion.   _____ Use a heating pad.

___1___ Use an ice pack.   _____ Use an inhaler.

  C Working Together **Tell your partner about a health problem.** Your partner will give you advice. Use the remedies below or give your own advice.

Health Problems
a cough
a headache
a backache
a toothache
a burn
a bad cold
a fever
a sore throat

Advice
Call the doctor.
Call the dentist.
Drink some hot tea.
Drink some soda.
Put ice on it.
Stay in bed.
Take aspirin.
Take ibuprofen.
Take some medicine.
Use a heating pad.

> I have a sore throat.

> Drink some hot tea.

Active Grammar

A **Read the directions.** Circle *must* or *must not*.

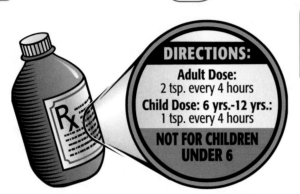

DIRECTIONS:
Adult Dose:
2 tsp. every 4 hours
Child Dose: 6 yrs.-12 yrs.:
1 tsp. every 4 hours
NOT FOR CHILDREN UNDER 6

| You | **must** | take this medicine with food. |
| Children | **must not** | take this medicine. |

must = It is necessary.
must not = Don't do it.

1. Adults **must** / **must not** take two teaspoons every four hours.

2. Adults **must** / **must not** take four teaspoons every two hours.

3. Children under six **must** / **must not** take this medicine.

Directions:
Adults: Take 2 capsules every 4–6 hours.
            Do not give to children.
            Do not use with alcohol.

4. An adult **must** / **must not** take this medicine every four to six hours.

5. Parents **must** / **must not** give this medicine to children.

6. A patient **must** / **must not** drink alcohol and take this medicine.

Directions:
      Take 1 capsule once a day.
      Take with food or milk.
      Do not drive; may cause drowsiness.

once a day = one time a day

7. A patient **must** / **must not** take one capsule a day.

8. Patients **must** / **must not** take this medicine with food or milk.

9. Patients **must** / **must not** drive if they take this medicine.

CULTURE NOTE
To get a prescription, you must see a doctor.

B **Read the label.** Complete the directions. Use *must* or *must not.*

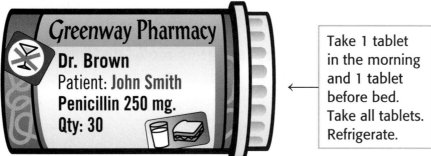

Greenway Pharmacy
Dr. Brown
Patient: John Smith
Penicillin 250 mg.
Qty: 30

Take 1 tablet
in the morning
and 1 tablet
before bed.
Take all tablets.
Refrigerate.

1. The patient ___must take___ (take) two tablets a day.

2. He _____ (eat) food with this medicine.

3. He _____ (drink) alcohol with this medicine.

4. He _____ (take) all the tablets.

5. He _____ (put) this medicine in the refrigerator.

C **Pronunciation: Medical Specialists Listen and repeat.**

CD3·TR34

1. a pediatrician **3.** an obstetrician / a gynecologist **5.** a psychologist

2. an allergist **4.** an optometrist **6.** a dermatologist

D **Match.**

___b___ **1.** A pediatrician **a.** checks your eyes.

_____ **2.** An allergist **b.** takes care of children.

_____ **3.** An obstetrician / **c.** talks to people about their
a gynecologist personal problems.

_____ **4.** An optometrist **d.** checks your skin.

_____ **5.** A psychologist **e.** takes care of women's health.

_____ **6.** A dermatologist **f.** helps people control their allergies.

E **Working Together   With a partner, write the names of three drugstores or pharmacies in your area.** Which one do you use?

1. _____

2. _____

3. _____

CD3·TR35

 A **Listen and label the people in the waiting room.**

~~Dr. Johnson~~	Mrs. Lee	Julia	Mr. Henderson
Mrs. Jacob	Mr. Green	Mr. Patel	Andy
Mrs. Jackson	Mrs. Rios	Miss Gonzalez	

B **Answer the questions.**

1. Who is getting a checkup?

2. Who has an allergy?

3. Who has a burn?

4. Who has a bad cough?

5. Who is working in the office?

6. Who is sick?

7. Who has a headache?

8. Who is getting a tetanus shot?

9. Who is a new patient?

tetanus shot

C Listen again. Read and circle.

CD3·TR35

1. Mrs. Jacob is the doctor.   True   ~~False~~
2. Mrs. Lee has a headache.   True   False
3. Mr. Green has a cold.   True   False
4. Mrs. Rios has allergies.   True   False
5. Julia's finger hurts.   True   False
6. Mr. Patel has a bad back.   True   False
7. Mrs. Jackson is a new patient.   True   False
8. Miss Gonzalez's throat hurts.   True   False
9. Andy has a stomachache.   True   False

D Complete.

allergies	~~bad cough~~	prescription
checkup	head	tetanus shot

1. Mrs. Lee has a _____ bad cough _____.
2. Mr. Green needs a _____.
3. Mr. Patel's _____ hurts.
4. Miss Gonzalez has _____.
5. She needs a _____.
6. Andy needs a _____.

E Circle.

1. The waiting room is busy because . . .
   a. it's late.   b. the doctor is away.   c. many people are sick.

2. Mrs. Jackson is going to fill out . . .
   a. a prescription.   b. a patient information form.   c. an application.

3. Mrs. Lee . . .
   a. is coughing.   b. is talking to the nurse.   c. is sneezing.

4. Miss Gonzalez needs a prescription for . . .
   a. allergies.   b. asthma.   c. a cold.

5. Andy feels . . .
   a. sick.   b. happy.   c. scared and nervous.

A Visit to the Doctor • **197**

A **Look at the chart.** How many hours of sleep do you need?

Age	Hours of sleep per night
Adults	7–8 hours
Teenagers	8–9 hours
Children	10–12 hours

B **Read.**

Tips for Getting a Good Night's Sleep

Is it difficult for you to fall asleep? Here are some ideas for a good night's sleep:

1. Try to go to bed and get up at the same time every day.

2. Take a warm shower or bath before you go to bed.

3. Relax before you close your eyes. Read a book or listen to soft music.

4. Don't eat late at night.

5. Make your room quiet and comfortable. Turn off the light.

6. Drink a cup of warm milk before you go to bed. Don't drink coffee or tea. Caffeine will keep you awake.

Everyone has trouble sleeping sometimes. If you have trouble sleeping for more than one month, see your doctor.

 C **Read each problem.** Give some good advice.

1. Joseph is 16 years old. He goes to school, plays soccer after school, works from 6:00 to 9:00, and then he does his homework until 12:00 A.M. He can't concentrate in school.

2. Maribel has many family problems. When she goes to bed, she thinks about her children, her husband, and her sisters. She can't sleep.

3. Mr. Andaba works from 3:00 to 11:00. When he gets home, he eats dinner. He goes to bed at 1:00, but he doesn't sleep well.

A **Read.**

I am 70 years old. I am a senior citizen. I think I am healthy. I am very active. I am retired, but I volunteer three days a week at the elementary school. I help the children read. I go to the park with my wife, and we walk two miles every morning. I go to the doctor every year for a checkup, and I see my dentist twice a year. I am a healthy person.

B **Complete the sentences about your lifestyle.**

1. I **am / am not** healthy.

2. I **always / sometimes / never** exercise. I exercise _____ time (s) a week.

3. I **sleep** _____ hours a night.

4. I go to the doctor **every year / twice a year.**   *OR* **I never get a checkup.**

5. I visit the dentist **once a year / twice a year.**   *OR* **I never go to the dentist**.

6. I need to   ❑ exercise more.

   ❑ sleep more.

   ❑ lose weight / gain weight.

   ❑ visit the doctor for a checkup.

> **WRITING NOTE**
> Check the plural nouns in your story. Most plural nouns end in *s*: *days, nights*. Some plural nouns are irregular: *children*.

C **Write a paragraph about your lifestyle.**

D **Sharing Our Stories** **Read your partner's story.** **Complete the sentences.**

1. _____ **always / sometimes / never** exercises.

2. _____ sleeps _____ hours a day.

CD3·TR36

A **Listen and practice with a partner.**

Receptionist: Hello, Dr. Walsh's office.

Patient: Hello, this is Mrs. Moreno.

Receptionist: Hello, Mrs. Moreno. How can I help you today?

Patient: My daughter is sick, and I need an appointment.

Receptionist: What's the problem?

Patient: She has a high fever and a sore throat.

Receptionist: Can you come in today at 2:00?

Patient: Yes, I can.

Receptionist: OK, Mrs. Moreno. See you at 2:00.

B **Working Together** **Complete the conversation with a partner.**

Receptionist: Hello, Dr. _____'s office.

Patient: Hello, this is _____.

Receptionist: Hello, _____. How can I help you today?

Patient: I'm sick, and I need an appointment.

Receptionist: What's the problem?

Patient: _____.

Receptionist: Can you come in today at _____?

Patient: _____.

Receptionist: OK, _____. See you at _____.

C **Working Together** **Act out the conversation in Exercise B.**

D **Complete.** Use your own information.

1. Dr. _____ is a good doctor.

2. Dr. _____ is a good dentist.

3. _____ is a good hospital.

4. _____ is a good drugstore.

CULTURE NOTE

When you visit a doctor's office for the first time, you must fill out a medical information form for yourself or for your child.

E **Complete the form.**

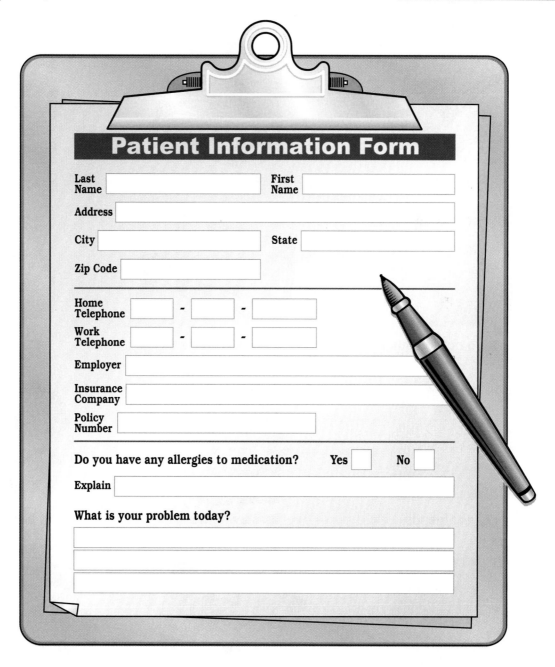

Patient Information Form

Last Name _____ First Name _____

Address _____

City _____ State _____

Zip Code _____

Home Telephone ___ - ___ - ___

Work Telephone ___ - ___ - ___

Employer _____

Insurance Company _____

Policy Number _____

Do you have any allergies to medication? Yes ☐ No ☐

Explain _____

What is your problem today?

_____

_____

_____

A **Listen and repeat.**

CD3·TR37

Daily Routines

1. get up early

2. do homework

3. go to the movies

4. go out to dinner

5. sleep late

6. rent a movie

7. visit friends

8. stay home

9. play soccer

10. watch TV

11. work

12. study

B **Listen and repeat.**

Celebrations

1. an anniversary

2. a birthday

3. a graduation

4. a wedding

C **Listen and repeat.**

Chores

1. iron clothes

2. do the laundry

3. do the shopping

4. vacuum the living room

D **Listen and repeat.**

Sports and Physical Activities

1. fish

2. dance

3. swim

4. camp

WORD PARTNERSHIPS	
	soccer
play	baseball
	volleyball
	fishing
go	dancing
	shopping

Word Builder

A **Match.** What is each person going to do?

_____e_____ **1.** Tom is driving to the river.

_____ **2.** The students are walking to the library.

_____ **3.** Mr. Lopez is at home. He's very tired.

_____ **4.** Tonight is Nancy and George's anniversary.

_____ **5.** We don't have any clean clothes.

_____ **6.** Jimmy and Chen want to see a movie.

_____ **7.** Ahmed needs a new suit for work.

_____ **8.** Julia and her friends want to exercise.

a. We're going to do the laundry.

b. He's going to go shopping at the mall.

c. They're going to go out to dinner.

d. They're going to go to the movies.

e. He's going to go fishing.

f. They're going to go to the gym.

g. He's going to stay home tonight.

h. They're going to study for a test.

B **Complete with the correct celebration.** You can use some words more than once.

| ~~anniversary~~ | birthday | graduation | wedding |

1. We're celebrating our twentieth ____anniversary____.

2. Tomorrow is my high school _____.

3. My niece's _____ is tomorrow. She's going to be 3 years old.

4. Our college _____ is going to be outside.

5. Jessica's husband gave her flowers and a necklace for their tenth _____.

6. My best friend is going to get married next Saturday.

The _____ is going to start at 2:00.

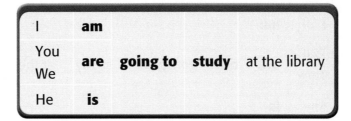

I	am			
You	are	going to	study	at the library
We				
He	is			

A **Complete with the future tense.**

1. We <u>are going to celebrate</u> (celebrate) our anniversary tonight.

2. The students _____ (take) a test next week.

3. My brother _____ (buy) a smaller car.

4. There _____ (be) a sale tomorrow.

5. Sarah _____ (look for) a new apartment.

6. It _____ (rain) next weekend.

7. The children _____ (eat) pizza for lunch.

8. I _____ (stay) home tomorrow.

B **Talk about your plans for the weekend.** Use *be going to*.

What are you going to do this Saturday?

I'm going to go to a birthday party.

C **Read and circle.**

1. The children are watching TV.   (Now)   Future   Everyday

2. He works at an express delivery company.   Now   Future   Everyday

3. They're going to move this year.   Now   Future   Everyday

4. She is cleaning her apartment.   Now   Future   Everyday

5. Belinda is going to make a salad for dinner.   Now   Future   Everyday

6. I always eat cereal and fruit for breakfast.   Now   Future   Everyday

I	am				
You They	are	not	going to	study	at the library.
She	is				

A Listen and write the sentences you hear.

CD3·TR41

1. I'm not going to watch TV tonight.

2. _____.

3. _____.

4. _____.

5. _____.

6. _____.

B Talk about the pictures.

He's going to see the dentist.

The dentist is going to take out his tooth.

1.

2.

3.

4.

5.

6.

7.

C **Pronunciation:** *going to* versus */gonna/* **Listen and repeat,** *going to* and */gonna/*.

CD3·TR42

1. Tom's going to sleep late tomorrow.

2. Mark and Ellen are going to celebrate their anniversary next week.

3. Are you going to do your homework tonight?

4. I'm going to do the laundry.

5. They aren't going to get up early on Sunday.

6. We're not going to watch TV.

> Do not write *gonna*. *Gonna* is only used in speaking.

D **Listen and complete.**

CD3·TR43

1. I ____'m going to vacuum____ my living room tomorrow.

2. The students _____ after class.

3. Some students _____ homework tonight.

4. My friend _____ this weekend.

5. My family and I _____ next month.

6. My brother _____ late tomorrow morning.

E **Practice saying the sentences in Exercise D.** Use *going to* and */gonna/*.

F **Working Together** **Plan your schedule for this week.** Complete the calendar with your activities for the next seven days. Share your schedule in a small group.

Sun.	Mon.	Tues.	Wed.	Thur.	Fri.	Sat.

A **Working Together** **Check (✔) your plans for this weekend.** Then, read your sentences to your partner. Check (✔) your partner's plans.

Weekend Plans	You		Your Partner	
	Yes	No	Yes	No
1. I'm going to get up early this weekend.				
2. I'm going to stay home this weekend.				
3. I'm going to work this weekend.				
4. I'm going to play a sport this weekend.				
5. I'm going to study English this weekend.				

B **Write sentences about you and your partner's plans for the weekend.**

1. _____

2. _____

3. _____

4. _____

5. _____

C **Working Together** **Find someone who . . .** Ask students questions about their future plans. If a student answers "Yes," write that student's name. If the student answers "No," ask another student.

> Yes, I am.
> No, I'm not.

Questions **Classmate**

1. Are you going to go camping this year? _____

2. Are you going to celebrate a birthday this month? _____

3. Are you going to exercise tomorrow? _____

4. Are you going to do the laundry this weekend? _____

5. Are you going to go dancing this weekend? _____

6. Are you going to eat at a restaurant this weekend? _____

7. Are you going to study English this weekend? _____

8. Are you going to speak English this weekend? _____

D **Write four sentences about your classmates.**

> He**'s going to** make a movie.
> She**'s going to** give a concert.

1. Marc Anthony, Singer

2. Carolina Herrera, Fashion Designer

3. Alex Pujols, Baseball Player

4. Yao Ming, Basketball Player

5. Barack and Michelle Obama, President and First Lady of the United States

6. Beyoncé, Singer/Actress

7. The Brazilian soccer team

8. Edwidge Danticat, Author

A Look at the picture and discuss the questions.

1. Where is the family going?

2. What are they going to take with them?

3. Is the dog going to go on the trip?

 ### B Listen and write each name on the correct person.

CD3•TR44

Al ~~Emily~~ Rico Linda Paula Pedro

C Listen again. Read and circle.

1. They're going to leave in an hour.	True	False
2. Linda is Emily's friend.	True	False
3. Paula is going to call the neighbors.	True	False
4. The neighbors are going to water the plants.	True	False
5. The dog is going to go with the family.	True	False
6. Al is going to use the surfboard.	True	False
7. Rico is going to take the surfboard with him.	True	False

D Read and circle the correct answers.

1. Who is Emily waiting for?

a. her cousin   **b.** her sister   **c.** her friend

2. Al is upset because they . . .

a. are going to be late.   **b.** have too many bags.   **c.** are ready.

3. Who's going to walk the dog?

a. Emily is.   **b.** The neighbors are.   **c.** Al is.

4. Where is Rico going to put the surfboard?

a. In the house.   **b.** On top of the car.   **c.** Inside the car.

5. Why aren't they going to leave now? Because Dad needs to . . .

a. get gas.   **b.** talk to the neighbor.   **c.** find his wallet.

E Complete with the correct verb form. Some verbs are negative.

1. The surfboard _____isn't going to fit_____ inside the car.

2. Rico _____ the surfboard on top of the car.

3. The family _____ a vacation.

4. The dog _____ on the trip.

5. The neighbors _____ the plants.

6. Emily's friend _____ with the family.

7. Pedro _____ in a car seat.

come
fit
go
put
ride
take
water

A **Circle your answers.**

1. I want to visit New York City.   Yes   No

2. I like to visit art museums.   Yes   No

3. There are many interesting   Yes   No
   museums in New York City.

B **Read about the Metropolitan Museum of Art.**

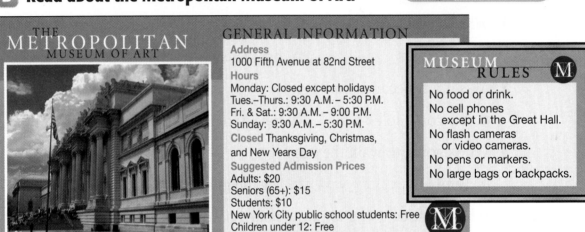

THE
METROPOLITAN
MUSEUM OF ART

GENERAL INFORMATION

Address
1000 Fifth Avenue at 82nd Street

Hours
Monday: Closed except holidays
Tues.–Thurs.: 9:30 A.M. – 5:30 P.M.
Fri. & Sat.: 9:30 A.M. – 9:00 P.M.
Sunday: 9:30 A.M. – 5:30 P.M.

Closed Thanksgiving, Christmas,
and New Years Day

Suggested Admission Prices
Adults: $20
Seniors (65+): $15
Students: $10
New York City public school students: Free
Children under 12: Free

MUSEUM RULES Ⓜ

No food or drink.
No cell phones
   except in the Great Hall.
No flash cameras
   or video cameras.
No pens or markers.
No large bags or backpacks.

C **Complete.**

1. The museum's address is _____.

2. The museum is open _____ through Sunday.

3. The museum is open from _____ A.M. to _____ P.M. on Fridays
   and Saturdays.

4. Children under 12 are _____.

5. Suggested admission for adults is _____.

6. Visitors cannot bring _____, _____,

   or _____.

A **Read.**

This weekend, I'm going to have a surprise party for my wife. We're going to have a cake, ice cream, and some punch. On Saturday morning, she's going to go to work. She doesn't know anything about the party. I'm going to clean our apartment. Then, I'm going to wrap her present in a special box. It's a pair of airline tickets to Brazil. Our children are going to decorate the apartment. They're going to give her presents, too. It's going to be a great party!

B **Write some notes about your weekend plans.**

Friday	Saturday	Sunday
	do laundry	

C **Write about your weekend plans.**

> **WRITING NOTE**
> Use a comma after a time expression at the beginning of a sentence.
> **On Saturday evening,** we're going to go to a movie.

D **Sharing Our Stories Read your partner's story.** Write two sentences about your partner's weekend plans.

A Read the calendar of events from this community newsletter.

JULY						
Sunday	**Monday**	**Tuesday**	**Wednesday**	**Thursday**	**Friday**	**Saturday**
		1 Farmer's Market 3–7 P.M. TS	**2** Adult Tennis 7 P.M. HS	**3** Kids Soccer 4 P.M. PK	**4** Independence Day: *Offices Closed* Rock Concert 7:30 P.M. Fireworks 9 P.M. PK	**5** Beach Bus 1 A.M. CHP
6 Music in the Park: *Salsa* Free Dance Lessons 3 P.M. 4–6 P.M. Concert PK	**7** Movie Night 8 P.M. LIB	**8** Farmer's Market 3–7 P.M. TS	**9** Adult Tennis 7 P.M. HS	**10** Kids Soccer 4 P.M. PK City Hall Meeting 7 P.M. CH	**11** Movie Night 9 P.M. PK	**12** Beach Bus 1 A.M. CHP

LEGEND	
LIB	- Public Library
CH	- City Hall
CHP	- City Hall Plaza
HS	- High School
PK	- Park
TS	- Train Station

A *legend* explains abbreviations in a map or chart.
Example: LIB - Library

B Answer the questions about the calendar.

1. Where is the Farmer's Market?

2. What day is the City Hall meeting? What time is the meeting?

3. When can you have free dance lessons?

4. What day is Kids Soccer?

5. Where can you see movies?

6. When can you listen to music in the park?

7. What time does the Beach Bus leave?

8. When are the fireworks?

C Working Together Read and practice the telephone conversation.

A: Hi, (B's name).

B: Hi, (A's name). What's up?

A: Nothing. Are you going to do anything on <u>Friday night</u>?

B: No. Why?

A: There's a <u>movie in the park</u> on <u>Friday night</u>.

B: That sounds like fun.

A: Good. Let's meet at <u>8:30</u>. <u>The movie starts at 9:00</u>.

B: Okay. See you then.

A: See you. Bye.

D Working Together Write a new conversation. Look at the calendar and choose an activity. Then, act out your new conversation for the class.

Unit 1

Possessive Adjectives

Possessive adjective	Noun	
My	name	is Adam.
Your	telephone number	is 555-1212.
His	teacher	is Miss Wilson.
Her	ID number	is 34345.
Our	classroom	is large.
Their	last name	is Brown.

> Note:
> A possessive adjective comes before a noun.

Present Tense of *Be*

FULL FORMS		
Subject	*Be*	
I	**am**	from Mexico.
You	**are**	a student.
He	**is**	a teacher.
She	**is**	from Haiti.
We	**are**	from Poland.
They	**are**	at school.
It	**is**	in Room 10.

CONTRACTIONS		
Subject	*Be*	
I**'m**		from Mexico.
You**'re**		a student.
He**'s**		a teacher.
She**'s**		from Haiti.
We**'re**		from Poland.
They**'re**		at school.
It**'s**		in Room 10.

> Notes:
> 1. We often use contractions when we speak.
> 2. We usually use full forms in writing.

Wh- Questions with *Be*

What / Where	*Be*	
What	is	your name?
Where	are	you from?
Where	is	he from?

> Notes:
> 1. Questions with *What* ask about things.
> 2. Questions with *Where* ask about places or locations.

Unit 2

Singular and Plural Nouns

REGULAR NOUNS	
Singular	Plural
a book	books
a pencil	pencils
a student	students
an eraser	erasers
an umbrella	umbrellas

IRREGULAR NOUNS	
Singular	Plural
a man	men
a woman	women
a child	children
a person	people

Notes:
1. Use an article with a singular noun.
2. Use *an* with nouns that begin with a vowel sound: *a, e, i, o,* and sometimes *u.*
3. Proper names do not take an article: *Tom, California, New York, Arizona.*

There is / There are

There	Be		
There	**is**	a book	on the desk.
There	**are**	books	on the desk.

Notes:
1. A sentence beginning with *There is* often tells about the location or existence of something.

   There is *a book on the desk.*

2. A sentence beginning with *There are* often tells how many.

   There are *twenty students in our class.*

3. We use *there* the first time we talk about a thing.

   There *is a book on the desk.* **It** *is a dictionary.* **There** *are many students in the classroom.* **They** *are from different countries.*

Yes / No Questions in the Present Tense with *Be*

QUESTIONS		
Be	Subject	
Is	this	your book?
Are	these	your books?

AFFIRMATIVE ANSWER		
Yes / No	Subject	*Be*
Yes,	it	**is.**
Yes,	they	**are.**

NEGATIVE ANSWER		
Yes / No	Subject	*Be*
No,	it	**isn't.**
No,	they	**aren't.**

Unit 3

Questions with *How old*

How old	*Be*	
How old	is	she?
How old	is	Tom?
How old	are	you?

Subject	*Be*	Number
She	is	27.
He	is	45.
I	am	14.

Adjectives

ADJECTIVES IN SENTENCES WITH *BE*		
Subject	*Be*	Adjective
I	am	**heavy.**
She	is	**old.**
They	are	**tall.**

ADJECTIVES IN SENTENCES WITH *HAVE*			
Subject	*Have / Has*	Adjective	Noun
I	have	**long**	hair.
She	has	**short**	hair.
They	have	**brown**	hair.

Notes:
1. Adjectives describe people, places, and things.
2. Adjectives are not plural, even if the noun is plural: ~~They are **talls**~~.   They are **tall**.

Yes / No Questions and Answers with *Be* and an Adjective in the Present

YES / NO QUESTIONS		
Be	Subject	Adjective
Am	I	tall?
Are	you	short?
Are	we	old?
Are	they	married?
Is	he	young?
Is	she	thin?
Is	it	heavy?

AFFIRMATIVE ANSWER		
Yes	Subject	*Be*
Yes,	you	**are.**
Yes,	I	**am.**
Yes,	we	**are.**
Yes,	they	**are.**
Yes,	he	**is.**
Yes,	she	**is.**
Yes,	it	**is.**

Notes:
1. Do not contract affirmative short answers. *Yes, he is.* NOT: ~~*Yes, he's.*~~

2. There is no contraction for *am not*, but the negative contraction for *I am not* is *I'm not*.

NEGATIVE ANSWERS		
No	Subject	*Be*
No,	you	**aren't.**
No,	I	**am not.**
No,	we	**aren't.**
No,	they	**aren't.**
No,	he	**isn't.**
No,	she	**isn't.**
No,	it	**isn't.**

NEGATIVE ANSWERS		
No	Subject + *Be*	*Not*
No,	you**'re**	**not.**
No,	I**'m**	**not.**
No,	we**'re**	**not.**
No,	they**'re**	**not.**
No,	he**'s**	**not.**
No,	she**'s**	**not.**
No,	it**'s**	**not.**

Unit 4

Where questions with *Be*

Where	*Be*	
Where	is	the pillow?
Where	are	the pillows?

Subject	*Be*	Preposition
It	is	**on** the bed.
They	are	**on** the sofa.

PREPOSITIONS

Subject	Be	
The book	is	**on** the table.
		under the table.
		next to the chair.
The books	are	**between** the computer and the printer.
		in the desk.

Unit 5

Present Continuous Tense

AFFIRMATIVE STATEMENTS

Subject	Be	-ing Form
I	**am**	study**ing**.
You	**are**	work**ing**.
We	**are**	sleep**ing**.
They	**are**	walk**ing**.
He	**is**	cook**ing**.
She	**is**	writ**ing**.
It	**is**	rain**ing**.

NEGATIVE STATEMENTS

Subject	Be + not	-ing Form
I	**am not**	study**ing**.
You	**aren't**	work**ing**.
We	**aren't**	sleep**ing**.
They	**aren't**	walk**ing**.
He	**isn't**	cook**ing**.
She	**isn't**	writ**ing**.
It	**isn't**	rain**ing**.

Notes:

1. The present continuous tense tells about an action that is happening now.

2. Some common present continuous time expressions are: *now, right now, at this moment.*

3. The negative contraction of *I am not* is *I'm not.*

4. Some verbs are usually not used in the present continuous tense. These verbs include *have, like, want, need, see, know,* and *be.* We use the present tense with these verbs.

Yes / No Questions in the Present Continuous Tense

YES / NO QUESTIONS

Be	Subject	-ing Form
Am	I	study**ing**?
Are	you	work**ing**?
Are	we	sleep**ing**?
Are	they	walk**ing**?
Is	he	cook**ing**?
Is	she	writ**ing**?
Is	it	rain**ing**?

SHORT ANSWERS

Affirmative	Negative
Yes, you **are**.	No, you **aren't**.
Yes, I **am**.	No, I'm **not**.
Yes, we **are**.	No, we **aren't**.
Yes, they **are**.	No, they **aren't**.
Yes, he **is**.	No, he **isn't**.
Yes, she **is**.	No, she **isn't**.
Yes, it **is**.	No, it **isn't**.

Unit 6

Or Questions

Be	Subject	Adjective	or	Adjective
Is	New York	small	**or**	large?
Are	the streets	clean	**or**	dirty?

Subject + *Be*	Adjective
It's	large.
They're	clean.

Adjective Word Order

Subject	Verb	Adjective	Noun
This	is	**a large**	city.
These	are	**large**	cities.

Notes:
1. Place the adjective before a noun.
2. Adjectives do not take the plural form.
   These are large cities. NOT: *These are ~~larges~~ cities.*

Unit 7

Prepositions

Subject	*Be*	Preposition
		on the corner of River Street and Pine Avenue.
		in front of the bank.
		in back of the drugstore.
The library	is	**next to** the park.
		between the hospital and the park.
		across from the police station.
		on River Street.

Giving Directions

Walk two blocks.
Turn right.
Turn left.

Note:
Use the base form of the verb to give directions.

Unit 8

Questions with *How much*

How much	Be	
How much	is	the printer?
How much	are	the batteries?

Subject + *Be*	Price
It's	$99.00.
They're	$7.95.

Notes:
1. *How much* questions ask about price.
2. For plural items, we often use *each* in the answer.
   How much are the donuts? They are $1.00. / They are $1.00 each.

Unit 9

Wh- Questions in the Present Continuous Tense

WH- QUESTIONS			
Wh- word	*Be*	Subject	*-ing* Form
What	am	I	wearing?
Where	are	you	driving?
What	are	we	doing?
Where	are	they	walking?
What	is	he	reading?
What	is	she	writing?

ANSWERS			
Subject	*Be*	*-ing* Form	
You	are	wearing	a coat.
I	am	driving	to the city.
We	are	studying	for a test.
They	are	walking	in the park.
He	is	reading	the newspaper.
She	is	writing	a letter.

Who Questions in the Present Continuous Tense

WHO QUESTIONS		
Who	*Be*	*-ing* Form
Who	is	studying?
Who	is	working?
Who	is	sleeping?
Who	is	walking?
Who	is	cooking?
Who	is	writing?

ANSWERS	
Subject	*Be*
I	am.
You	are.
He	is.
She	is.
We	are.
They	are.

Notes:
1. The word *Who* asks questions about people.
2. *Who* takes a singular verb. Who **is** *sitting in the class? The students* **are**.

Unit 10

How much questions

How much	*Be*	
How much	is	the shirt?
How much	are	the jeans?

Subject + *Be*	Price
It's	$24.00.
They're	$39.98.

Notes:
1. *How much* questions ask about price.

WEATHER		
Wh	*Be*	
What	is	the weather?
How	is	the weather?

Subject + *Be*	
It's	sunny and hot.
It's	windy.

Unit 11

Simple Present Tense

AFFIRMATIVE STATEMENTS		
Subject	Verb	
I	work	every day.
You	work	at night.
We	work	in the morning.
They	work	part time.
He	works	full time.
She	works	on the weekends.
It	works	every day.

NEGATIVE STATEMENTS		
Subject	do not / does not	Verb
I	don't	work.
You	don't	work.
We	don't	work.
They	don't	work.
He	doesn't	work.
She	doesn't	work.
It	doesn't	work.

Notes:

1. The simple present tense tells about a repeated or routine action.

2. The present tense tells about facts that are true all the time.
   I live in the city. I like my class.

3. In affirmative statements, *he, she,* and *it* use *s* on the verb.

Common Time Expressions in the Present Tense

in	*on*	*every*	*at*	*from . . . to . . .*
in the morning	on Monday	every day	at 4:00	from Monday to Friday
in the afternoon	on Friday	every morning	at noon	from 1:00 to 3:00
in the evening	on the weekend	every evening	at midnight	
		every night	at night	

Unit 12

Adverbs of Frequency

I **always** drink water on hot days.
I **sometimes** drink coffee in the morning.
I **never** drink coffee at night.

Notes:

1. *Always* means 100% of the time.

2. *Sometimes* means about 50% of the time.

3. *Never* means 0%. You never do this action.

Unit 13

Yes / No Questions and Answers in the Simple Present Tense

YES / NO QUESTIONS		
Do / Does	Subject	Verb
Do	I	work?
Do	you	work?
Do	we	work?
Do	they	work?
Does	he	work?
Does	she	work?
Does	it	work?

SHORT ANSWERS	
Affirmative	Negative
Yes, you **do**.	No, you **don't**.
Yes, I **do**.	No, I **don't**.
Yes, we **do**.	No, we **don't**.
Yes, they **do**.	No, they **don't**.
Yes, he **does**.	No, he **doesn't**.
Yes, she **does**.	No, she **doesn't**.
Yes, it **does**.	No, it **doesn't**.

Wh- Questions in the Simple Present Tense

WH- QUESTIONS			
Wh- word	*Be*	Subject	Verb
When	do	I	leave?
Where	do	you	work?
What	do	we	wear?
When	do	they	eat?
Where	does	he	work?
What time	does	she	get up?

ANSWERS		
Subject	Verb	
You	leave	at 2:00.
I	work	at the hotel.
We	wear	uniforms.
They	eat	at 7:00.
He	works	at the bank.
She	gets up	at 6:00.

Who questions in the Simple Present Tense

WHO QUESTIONS		
Who	Verb + *s*	
Who	works	in a store?
Who	gets	benefits?
Who	wears	a uniform?
Who	has	a difficult job?
Who	works	at night?
Who	gets	tips?

ANSWERS	
Subject	*Do*
I	**do**.
You	**do**.
We	**do**.
They	**do**.
He	**does**.
She	**does**.

Notes:
1. The word *Who* asks questions about people.

2. *Who* takes a singular verb. Who **works** full time? Nelson does. Who **works** full time? Nelson and Victor do.

Unit 14

Must / Must not

You	**must**	take this medicine with food.
Children	**must not**	take this medicine.

Note:
1. *Must* means that something is necessary.
2. *Must not* means that something is against the law. It is not permitted.

Unit 15

Future Tense Statements

AFFIRMATIVE STATEMENTS			
Subject	*Be*	*Going To*	Verb
I	**am**	**going to**	study.
You	**are**	**going to**	rent a movie.
We	**are**	**going to**	stay home.
They	**are**	**going to**	visit friends.
He	**is**	**going to**	play soccer.
She	**is**	**going to**	watch TV.
It	**is**	**going to**	rain.

NEGATIVE STATEMENTS			
Subject	*Be + Not*	*Going To*	Verb
I	**am not**	**going to**	study.
You	**aren't**	**going to**	rent a movie.
We	**aren't**	**going to**	stay home.
They	**aren't**	**going to**	visit friends.
He	**isn't**	**going to**	play soccer.
She	**isn't**	**going to**	watch TV.
It	**isn't**	**going to**	rain.

Note:
The future tense tells about actions that are going to happen tomorrow, next week, or some time in the future.

Common Time Expressions in the Future Tense

in	*next*	*this*	Adverbs
in a minute	next Sunday	this morning	today
in a few minutes	next week	this afternoon	tomorrow
in an hour	next weekend	this evening	tomorrow morning
in two days	next month		tonight
in a week	next year		soon
in a month			later
in a year			
in 2020			

Plural Nouns

1. For most nouns, add an -*s*.
boy-boys   *store-stores*   *student-students*

2. If a noun ends with a consonant and a *y*, change the *y* to *i*, and add -*es*.
city-cities   *dictionary-dictionaries*   *baby-babies*

3. If a noun ends with *sh, ch, x,* or *z*, add -*es*.
box-boxes   *dress-dresses*   *watch-watches*

Present Continuous Verbs

1. For most verbs, add -*ing*.
walk-walking   *play-playing*   *eat-eating*

2. If a verb ends in *e*, drop the *e* and add -*ing*.
write-writing   *come-coming*   *drive-driving*

3. If a verb ends in a consonant + vowel + consonant, double the final consonant and add -*ing*.
sit-sitting   *run-running*   *put- putting*

Present Tense: Third Person

1. For most verbs, add -*s*.
make-makes   *call-calls*   *sleep-sleeps*

2. If a verb ends with a consonant and a *y*, change the *y* to *i*, and add -*es*.
try-tries   *cry-cries*   *apply-applies*

3. If a verb ends with *sh, ch, x,* or *z*, add -*es*.
wash-washes   *watch-watches*   *fix-fixes*

4. These verbs are irregular in the third person.
have-has   *do-does*

For Page 76, Exercise C

Student 1: Read Questions 1-6 to your partner.

  1. Is this classroom large or small?

  2. Is the classroom clean or dirty?

  3. Is this school busy or quiet?

  4. Are the students friendly?

  5. Are the books boring?

  6. Is the classroom hot today?

Student 2: Listen and write your answers. Then, read Questions 7-12 to your partner.

  7. Is this city in the mountains?

  8. Is the traffic heavy now?

  9. Is the weather humid or dry today?

  10. Is this city noisy or quiet?

  11. Are the streets in this city clean or dirty?

  12. Are the parks beautiful?

Audio Scripts

Unit 1

CD1·TR4
(Page 4)

B **Listen and write the letter you hear.**
1. C **2.** F **3.** H **4.** W **5.** L **6.** Z **7.** S **8.** G **9.** J

CD1·TR8
(Page 8)

C **Listen and complete.** Listen for the long form or the short form.
1. I am from Mexico. **2.** She's from Alaska. **3.** They're from Chile. **4.** We're from Cameroon.
5. He is from Ukraine. **6.** I'm from Italy. **7.** It is from Vietnam. **8.** You're from Colombia.

CD1·TR9
(Page 11)

A **The Big Picture: My Classmates**
Hi. My name is Tomás. I'm a student in English 1. I'm in class now. Here are four students in my class. This is Hiro. He's from Japan. This is Erica. She's from Mexico. This is Marie. She's from Haiti. This is Jenny. She's from Hong Kong. And this is me. I'm from Peru.

CD1·TR10
(Page 11)

C **Listen and write the answers.**
1. Who is from Peru? **2.** Who is from Japan? **3.** Who is from Mexico? **4.** Where is Marie from?
5. Where is Jenny from? **6.** Where are you from?

CD1·TR11
(Page 11)

D **Listen.** Write the number next to the correct answer.
1. What's your name? **2.** Where are you from? **3.** What's his name? **4.** Where is he from?
5. What's her name? **6.** Where is she from?

CD1·TR13
(Page 14)

B **Listen and write the numbers.**
a. six **b.** eleven **c.** zero **d.** eighteen **e.** two **f.** fifteen
g. three **h.** ten **i.** seventeen **j.** twenty **k.** four **l.** nine
m. thirteen **n.** eight **o.** twelve

CD1·TR14
(Page 14)

C **Listen and write the words for the numbers.**
a. ten **b.** six **c.** eleven **d.** three **e.** twelve
f. eighteen **g.** twenty **h.** one **i.** seventeen

CD1·TR16
(Page 15)

B **Listen and write.**
a. 555-3231 **b.** 555-3692 **c.** 800-555-4242 **d.** 201-555-4413
e. 555-3692 **f.** 555-7548 **g.** 619-555-7042 **h.** 813-555-1624

Unit 2

CD1·TR19
(Page 18)

B **Listen and complete.**
1. Is this your dictionary? Yes, it is. Thank you.
2. Is this your pen? Yes, it is. Thank you.
3. Is this your piece of paper? No, it isn't.
4. Is this your notebook? Yes, it is. Thank you.
5. Is this your pencil sharpener? No, it isn't.

CD1·TR21
(Page 20)

A **Pronunciation: Plural nouns** Listen and circle.
1. a pencil **2.** students **3.** teachers **4.** a man **5.** a map
6. dictionaries **7.** an eraser **8.** a notebook **9.** classrooms **10.** women

CD1·TR22
(Page 23)

B **Listen and circle Desk 1 or Desk 2.**
1. There is a notebook on this desk.
2. There are pencils on this desk.
3. There is a dictionary on this desk.
4. There is a pencil sharpener on this desk.

5. There is a computer on this desk.
6. There are four textbooks on this desk.
7. There is a piece of paper on this desk.
8. There are two pens on this desk.

CD1·TR23
(Page 24)

The Big Picture: The Classroom

I am a student in English 1. My classroom is on the second floor in Room 204. There are ten students in my class. There are four men and six women. We are from different countries. There are five students from Mexico. There are two students from Vietnam. There is one student from El Salvador, one from India, and one from the Philippines.

Our room is small. There is a big table in the front for the teacher: There are twelve desks for the students. There is a chalkboard on the wall. There are two maps on the wall, one of the United States and one of the world.

Our teacher is Mr. Wilson. We like our teacher, and we like our class.

CD1·TR24
(Page 25)

Listen and circle.

1. The classroom is in Room 208.
2. There are twelve students in this class.
3. There are ten men in this class.
4. There are six women in this class.
5. There are four children in this class.
6. There are five students from India.
7. There is one student from El Salvador.
8. The room is small.
9. There are two maps on the wall.

CD1·TR25
(Page 25)

Listen. If the information is correct, write the sentence. If the information is wrong, put an X.

1. The teacher is a woman.
2. The classroom is in Room 204.
3. There are five students from Mexico.
4. There are ten women in this class.
5. There are ten students in this class.
6. There is a table for the teacher.
7. There is a computer in this class.
8. There is a board in the room.

Unit 3

CD1·TR30
(Page 31)

Listen and circle the name of the correct person.

1. He is Sylvia's husband.
2. She is Sylvia's mother.
3. He is Sylvia's brother.
4. She is Eric's sister.
5. She is Annie's aunt.
6. He is Pedro's father.
7. He is Annie's uncle.
8. She is Annie and Eric's grandmother.
9. He is Elisa's nephew.

CD1·TR32
(Page 34)

Listen. Number the photographs. Then, listen again and write the relationships and ages.

Conversation 1
A: This is my daughter, Carmen, and her little boy. His name is Dennis, and he's two years old. He's our first grandchild.
B: How old is Carmen?
A: She's 35.

Conversation 2
A: This is my son, Brian. He's three. And this is our daughter, Erica.
B: How old is Erica?
A: She's six.
B: That's a cute picture.

Conversation 3
A: This is my daughter, Gwen. She's 25. And this is her husband, Ellis. He's 28. They live in Florida.
B: Do they have any children?
A: No, they don't.

CD1·TR33
(Page 36) **Listen and write the questions.** Ask a partner the questions.

1. Are you at school?
2. Are you single?
3. Are you short?
4. Are you from China?
5. Are you young?

CD1·TR34
(Page 38) **The Big Picture: A Family Photo**

A: I have the pictures from the party last week.
B: Oh, yes, your mom's birthday party. Let me see.
A: Here's a picture of everyone.
B: Oh, that's you and Steve. And your two little girls. Which one is Emily and which one is Kim?
A: Emily is five. She has long hair. And Kim is six. She has short hair.
B: Now, that's your mom and dad. Right? In the middle?
A: Yes. That's mom. It's her birthday. She's 55 years old. And that's dad, next to her.
B: Oh, your dad has a moustache?
A: Yes. He has a moustache. At one time, he had curly hair, but now he's bald.
B: Who's this?
A: These are my sisters. I have two sisters. This is my sister, Joanne. She's 21. And next to her, that's my sister, Mary. She's 23.
B: Joanne and Mary look a lot alike.
A: I know. They're tall and they both have dark, curly hair. But Joanne is a little heavy, and Mary is very thin.
B: Are your sisters married?
A: No, I'm the only one who is married.
B: And who's this?
A: That's my brother, Andy.
B: Oh, you have a brother?
A: Yes, I have a brother. Andy is the baby of the family. He's 18.
B: He looks like your dad.
A: Hmm. You're right.
B: That's a great picture.

CD1·TR36
(Page 39) **Listen and complete.** Then, put a period (.) or a question mark (?) at the end of each sentence.

1. She is old.
2. Is he young?
3. Is it heavy?
4. It is tall.
5. She is thin.
6. Is he tall?
7. Is she short?
8. He is heavy.

CD1·TR39
(Page 42) **Listen and write.**

1. January 4, 2005
2. February 11, 1992
3. April 17, 2010
4. July 25, 1990
5. August 18, 2015
6. September 7, 1964
7. November 30, 1999
8. December 25, 2000

Unit 4

CD1·TR42
(Page 48) **Listen and write each question.** Then, look at the picture and write the answer.

1. Where is the end table?
2. Where are the books?
3. Where is the lamp?
4. Where is the rug?
5. Where are the pillows?
6. Where is the mirror?

CD1·TR43
(Page 51) **Look at the picture on page 50 and listen to the conversation.** Write the missing questions.

Tom: Where is my cell phone?
Sara: Is it on the coffee table?
Tom: No, it isn't.
Sara: Is it on the desk?
Tom: No, it isn't.
Sara: Is it on the floor?
Tom: Yes, here it is!

CD1·TR44
(Page 51) **B** **Listen.** Write the missing questions.

Tom:	Where are my keys?		**Tom:**	No, they aren't.
Sara:	Are they under the coffee table?		**Sara:**	Are they next to the computer?
Tom:	No, they aren't.		**Tom:**	Yes, here they are!
Sara:	Are they on the sofa?			

CD1·TR45
(Page 52) **B** **The Big Picture: A Messy Bedroom**

Kathy: Hi, Mom.
Mom: Hi, Kathy. Doing your homework?
Kathy: Yes, I have a lot of homework.
Mom: How's your room?
Kathy: How's my room?
Mom: Yes, is it clean? Is it neat?
Kathy: Yes, Mom. My room is perfect.
Mom: Are your clothes on the floor?
Kathy: Are my clothes on the floor?
Mom, my clothes are in the closet.
Mom: And your shoes and your boots?
Kathy: They're in the closet, too.
Mom: And your desk?
Kathy: My desk is perfect.
Mom: Are your books and papers on the floor?
Kathy: Mom, my books and papers are on the desk.
Mom: Good! Grandma is coming today.
And you know Grandma!
Kathy: Oh, no! Grandma is coming?! When?
Mom: In about 10 minutes.
Kathy: Thanks, Mom.
Mom: Bye, Kathy. See you in a few minutes.

CD1·TR46
(Page 53) **C** **Listen to the questions.** Write the number of the question next to Kathy's answer.

1. Hi, Kathy. Doing your homework?
2. Is your room clean? Is it neat?
3. Are your clothes on the floor?
4. And your shoes and your boots?
5. Are your books and papers on the floor?

CD1·TR47
(Page 56) **B** **Listen to each address and repeat.**

a. 56 Main Street
b. 37 Maple Street
c. 244 Second Street
d. 872 Central Avenue
e. 1524 Park Avenue
f. 2159 North Avenue

CD1·TR48
(Page 56) **C** **Listen.** Complete the addresses. Then, repeat the addresses with a partner.

a. 73 North Avenue
b. 66 Maple Street
c. 143 Central Avenue
d. 861 Park Avenue
e. 9924 First Street
f. 3285 Main Street

Unit 5

CD1·TR51
(Page 60) **C** **Listen and circle the form you hear.**

1. He is walking.
2. She's cleaning.
3. I'm making lunch.
4. You're driving.
5. They are watching TV.
6. We are studying.

CD1·TR52
(Page 64) **A** **Listen and complete.**

A: Hello.
A: I'm at home. I'm in the kitchen.
A: I'm cooking dinner.

B: Hi, Jenny. It's Sarah. Where are you?
B: What are you doing?
B: Okay. I'll call you later.

230 · Audio Scripts

B **Listen and complete.**

A: Hello.
A: I'm at the gym.
A: I'm working out.

B: Hi, Alex. It's Ben. Where are you?
B: What are you doing?
B: Okay. I'll call you later.

A **The Big Picture: Mom's on the phone!**

Tommy: Hello.
Mom: Hi, Tommy. This is Mommy.
Tommy: Hi, Mommy. Are you at work?
Mom: Yes, I'm a little late. What are you doing? Are you doing your homework?
Tommy: No, I'm not. I'm watching TV.
Mom: Where's Brian? Is he doing his homework?
Tommy: Brian's in the living room. He's playing video games.
Mom: And Katie? Where's Katie?
Tommy: She's in her bedroom.
Mom: Good! Is she doing her homework?
Tommy: No, Mom. She's talking on the phone with her boyfriend.
Mom: Where's Daddy? Is he cooking dinner?
Tommy: Daddy's in the living room. He's sleeping.
Mom: I'm coming home right now.

D **Listen and write short answers.**

1. Is Mom at home?
2. Is she talking to Tommy?
3. Is Tommy doing his homework?
4. Is Brian doing his homework?

5. Is Brian playing video games?
6. Is Dad cooking dinner?
7. Is Katie doing her homework?

A **Listen and look at the message.**

A: Hello.
B: Can I speak with Carlos?
A: I'm sorry. He's not here. Can I take a message?
B: This is Steve Carson.
A: Steve Carson?
B: Please ask him to call me. My number is 555-8341.
A: Please repeat that.
B: 555-8341.
A: Okay.

B **Listen to two phone calls.** Take the messages.

CALL 1
A: Hello.
B: Can I speak with Maya?
A: I'm sorry. She's not here. Can I take a message?
B: This is Mary Lyons.
A: Mary Lyons?
B: Yes. Please ask her to call me. My number is 555-6672.
A: Please repeat that.
B: 555-6672.
A: Okay.

CALL 2
A: Hello.
B: May I speak with Mr. Pano?
A: I'm sorry. He's not here. Can I take a message?
B: This is Adam Madison.
A: Adam?
B: Adam Madison.
A: Please spell that.
B: M-A-D-I-S-O-N. Please ask him to call me. My number is 555-9143.
A: Please repeat that.
B: 555-9143.
A: Okay.

Unit 6

CD2·TR4
(Page 75) **Listen and point to each city on the map.** Listen again and repeat.

1. Seattle, Washington
2. San Francisco, California
3. Las Vegas, Nevada
4. Phoenix, Arizona
5. Detroit, Michigan
6. Chicago, Illinois
7. San Antonio, Texas
8. Boston, Massachusetts
9. New York, New York
10. Miami, Florida

CD6·TR5
(Page 77) **Listen and complete.**

Male: What city do you want to visit?
Female: I want to visit Miami.
Male: Why do you want to go there?
Female: I want to visit Miami because it's sunny and beautiful.
Male: Well, *I* want to visit New York City.
Female: Why do you want to go there?
Male: Because it's exciting. There are so many things to do!

CD2·TR6
(Page 80) **The Big Picture: Chicago, Illinois**

Chicago, Illinois

Chicago, Illinois is one of the largest cities in the U.S. It's in the midwest of the country next to Lake Michigan. The summers are hot, and the winters are cold, so visit Chicago in the spring or in the fall.

There are many interesting places to visit. Many places are in busy downtown Chicago. If you like art, go to the Art Institute of Chicago. There are many famous paintings there. For children, the Brookfield Zoo is a fun place to visit. But, if you like something different, go to one of Chicago's blues clubs. You'll see great blues musicians. Maybe you'll want to dance.

If you like sports, Chicago is a great city. There are seven professional teams in Chicago. Wrigley Field, a baseball park, is the oldest baseball park in the United States. It's the home of the Chicago Cubs baseball team.

Do you watch TV talk shows? Then, you know Oprah Winfrey. Millions of people watch her TV show every afternoon. If you go to Chicago, maybe you can watch the Oprah show live! Finally, the 44th President of the United States—Barack Obama— worked in Chicago.

So, when do you want to visit Chicago? Chicago is waiting for you.

CD2·TR8
(Page 85) **Listen and write the population.**

1. Seattle, Washington: 594,210
2. Phoenix, Arizona: 1,552,259
3. San Jose, California: 939,899
4. Boston, Massachusetts: 590,763
5. Chicago, Illinois: 2,836,658
6. Honolulu, Hawaii: 371,657
7. Dallas, Texas: 1,240,499
8. Greensboro, North Carolina: 258,671

Unit 7

CD2·TR11
(Page 88) **Listen and complete the map.**

1. **A:** Where's the bakery?
   B: It's on Main Street, next to the park.
2. **A:** Where's the supermarket?
   B: It's across from the post office.
3. **A:** Where's the shoe store?
   B: It's on Main Street, across from the drugstore.
4. **A:** Where's the bookstore?
   B: It's next to the shoe store.
5. **A:** Where's the library?
   B: It's on Maple Avenue. It's behind the post office.
6. **A:** Where's the bank?
   B: It's on the corner of Main Street and First Street.
7. **A:** Where's the coffee shop?
   B: It's next to the post office.
8. **A:** Where's the Laundromat?
   B: It's on the corner of Second Street and Maple Avenue.

Listen and write the locations on the map on page 90.

1. **A:** Where's City Hall?
   B: Walk two blocks to Broad Street. Turn left. City Hall is on your right.
2. **A:** Where's the post office?
   B: Walk two blocks to Broad Street. Turn left. The post office is on your left.

3. **A:** Where's the hospital?
   B: Walk three blocks to the first traffic light. Turn right. The hospital is on your left.
4. **A:** Where's the aquarium?
   B: Walk four blocks to the second traffic light. That's Clark Street. Turn right. The aquarium is on your left.

The Big Picture: Downtown

It's a busy afternoon downtown. People are busy, and the stores are busy, too. Oh, look! There's an accident at the intersection of Smith Street and North Main Street. Mr. Thomas works at the bakery, and he drives the delivery truck. He's talking to the other driver. Over in the park, Elena is watching the children. The children are playing on the swings. They're having a good time. There's a coffee shop on North Main Street. There are two tables in front of the coffee shop. Joseph is sitting at a table. He's reading the newspaper and drinking a cup of coffee. Jane is sitting at the other table. She's reading a good book. Mark is the waiter. He's bringing Jane some ice cream. Uh, oh. Mrs. Lee is running to her car. Officer Ortiz is standing next to her car. He's writing her a ticket. Oh, how wonderful! Michael and Luisa are in front of City Hall. I think they're getting married today.

Listen and circle.

1. Who is watching the children?
2. Who is getting married?
3. Who is standing at the corner of Smith Street and North Main Street?
4. Who is running?

5. Who is working at the coffee shop?
6. Who is reading a book?
7. Who is drinking a cup of coffee?
8. Who is writing a ticket?

Unit 8

Listen and write the amount.

a. two cents
b. ten cents
c. seventeen cents

d. twenty-five cents
e. thirty-eight cents
f. forty-nine cents

g. fifty cents
h. sixty-nine cents
i. ninety-eight cents

Listen and write the amount.

a. a dollar
b. a dollar twenty-five
c. two dollars and fifty cents
d. three seventy-five
e. fifteen dollars and eight cents

f. seventy-nine twenty-five
g. one hundred fifty-seven dollars and sixty-two cents
h. two hundred thirty dollars and ninety-nine cents
i. four hundred fifty-seven dollars and twenty-four cents

Circle the number you hear.

a. 13   **b.** 40   **c.** 15   **d.** 60   **e.** 70   **f.** $18   **g.** $19   **h.** $13
i. $15   **j.** $19   **k.** $14.14   **l.** $17.20   **m.** $16.16   **n.** 18.75   **o.** 10.50

The Big Picture: I need a desk

Katrina: I can't study. It's too noisy.
Fabio: You can study in the bedroom. It's quiet in the bedroom.
Katrina: Yes, but I don't have a desk or a chair.
Fabio: Let's go to the office supply store tomorrow. You're right. You need a desk and a chair in the bedroom.
Katrina: And I need a light. It's too dark in the bedroom. I need a good light for reading.
Fabio: Anything else?
Katrina: I have my books and notebooks. But I need some folders.
Fabio: When we're there, I'm going to look at shredders.

CD2·TR24
(Page 109) **Listen to the conversation.** Then, write the items that Katrina and Fabio buy. Write the prices.

Katrina:	They have lots of desks.
Fabio:	This one is nice.
Katrina:	I think it's too big.
Fabio:	How about this one. It's a good price, $99.
Katrina:	But that one is too small. And it doesn't have a drawer.
Fabio:	This one is the right size, and it has a drawer.
Katrina:	I like that one. How much is it?
Fabio:	Not bad. It's $119.
Katrina:	Now, I need a chair.
Fabio:	Try out a lot of them. You want to find one that's comfortable. Do you want one with arms?
Katrina:	Well, I don't like this one. It's too big for me and it isn't comfortable.
Fabio:	How about this one?
Katrina:	I like it. And it's a good price, $69. Okay, we have the desk, a chair, and now we need a lamp.
Fabio:	How much is this lamp?
Katrina:	It's on sale for $19.
Fabio:	Good! Let's buy it. We did well today. The shredder is on sale for $20, and your folders are $4. Let's go to the checkout counter.

CD2·TR25
(Page 109) **Listen and write the responses.**

1. **A:** This desk is nice.   **B:** It's too big.
2. **A:** How about this desk?   **B:** It's too small.
3. **A:** This one is the right size.   **B:** Yes, I like that one.
4. **A:** Do you like this chair?   **B:** It's too big for me.
5. **A:** How about this one?   **B:** It isn't comfortable.
6. **A:** How about this one?   **B:** I like it. And it's a good price.
7. **A:** How much is the lamp?   **B:** It's on sale for $19.

Unit 9

CD2·TR27
(Page 120) **Listen to each question.** Write the name of the correct person.

1. Who is looking at the bus schedule?
2. Who is listening to music?
3. Who is standing in back of Roberto?
4. Who is talking?
5. Who is running to the bus stop?
6. Who is reading a book?
7. Who is talking on a cell phone?
8. Who is playing a video game?
9. Who is carrying two large shopping bags?

CD2·TR28
(Page 122) **The Big Picture: The Train Station**

1. Who is running for the train?
2. Who is carrying a briefcase?
3. Who is reading a newspaper?
4. Who is talking on a cell phone?
5. Who is looking at the clock?
6. Who is drinking a cup of coffee?
7. Who is buying a ticket?

CD2·TR29
(Page 123) **Listen to each sentence.** Who is talking?

1. Hi! How are you? How's your new job?
2. I'd like a round-trip ticket to New York.
3. Good-bye! I'll miss you!
4. Is this the train to Washington?
5. I'm at the station now and my train is at 2:30. I'll call you again when I get to Trenton.

CD2·TR30
(Page 123) **Listen to the story and complete the questions.**

Emily is standing next to the train and saying good-bye to her boyfriend. She's very sad, and she's crying. Emily is unhappy because her boyfriend is leaving for the army. He's standing on the train and waving good-bye. Emily is 18, and she's a senior in high school. Tom is 20 and he is going into the army. He is reporting for duty in New York. Tom is sad about Emily, but he's excited about his future. He's saying, "Don't cry, Emily. I'll call you when I get to camp. We can e-mail each other. I'll see you in eight weeks."

Listen. What is Amy wearing? Write the letter of the correct picture.

1. She's wearing a blue dress.
2. She's wearing beige shorts.
3. She's wearing black pants.
4. She's wearing a big white belt.
5. She's wearing a green shirt.

6. She's wearing a white blouse.
7. She's wearing sneakers.
8. She's wearing a green jacket.
9. She's wearing white sandals.
10. She's wearing a white sweater.

  Listen to the weather. Find the city and write the temperature on the map.

1. Find Boston. It's cold in Boston today. It's snowing. The temperature is 20 degrees.
2. Find New York. It's cloudy and cold in New York today. The temperature is 35 degrees.
3. Find Miami. It's sunny and hot in Miami. The temperature is 90 degrees.
4. Find Houston. It's sunny and warm in Houston today. The temperature is 70 degrees.
5. Find San Diego. The weather is warm in San Diego all year. It's sunny and 75 degrees.
6. Find San Francisco. It's raining today in San Francisco. It's cool. The temperature is 55 degrees.
7. Find Seattle. It's raining in Seattle, too. It's 50 degrees in Seattle. You will need your umbrella and raincoat.
8. Find Denver. It's snowing in Denver today. It's 30 degrees.
9. Find Chicago. It's cloudy and cold in Chicago today. It's very windy. The temperature is 25 degrees.

  Josh needs a new pair of shoes. Listen to the story and number the pictures from 1 to 8.

1. Josh needs a new pair of shoes for work. He's walking into a shoe store.
2. Josh is looking at all the shoes. He's picking up a nice pair of black shoes.
3. He's sitting down and putting on the shoes.
4. Josh is standing. He doesn't like the shoes. They're too tight.
5. Now, Josh is trying on another pair of shoes. The shoes are a larger size.
6. He is looking in the mirror. He likes the shoes. They're the right size.
7. Josh is standing at the counter and giving the box of shoes to the clerk.
8. Josh is paying for the shoes. The shoes are $49. He's giving his credit card to the clerk.

  Listen and complete the conversation.

Clerk: Hello. Can I help you?
Customer: Yes. I'm looking for a shirt.
Clerk: What size?
Customer: Medium.
Clerk: The shirts are here.
Customer: I like this shirt. How much is it?
Clerk: It's $50. But today it's on sale for $25.
Customer: Great. I'll take it.

B **Listen and complete the conversation.**

Clerk: Hello. Can I help you?
Customer: Yes. I'm looking for a pair of gloves.
Clerk: What size?
Customer: Extra large.
Clerk: Here they are.
Customer: I like these gloves. How much are they?
Clerk: They're usually $30. But today they're on sale for $19.
Customer: Great. I'll take them.

CD2·TR39
(Page 138)

The Big Picture: The Clothing Store

Monica is from Cuba. Cuba is an island in the Caribbean. It's hot there all year. Now Monica is living in Boston. Monica came to the United States in May. She liked the weather in Boston in May, June, July, and August. It was sunny and hot. September was warm, and Monica was comfortable. But now it is December. Monica can't believe the weather! It's very cold. It's 30 degrees. Her friends tell her, "This isn't cold yet! In January, it's going to be colder. And it's going to snow soon." Monica is at the clothing store with her sister, Lydia. Monica needs warm clothes. She needs a coat. She needs a hat and gloves, too. She is also going to buy a sweater. Monica is standing in front of the mirror. She's trying on coats. She isn't comfortable. She's saying, "This coat feels so heavy."

CD2·TR40
(Page 139)

Listen and complete the conversations.

1. **Monica:** I don't like this weather. It's too cold.
   Lydia: It's only December. It isn't cold yet. Wait until January!
2. **Lydia:** Here's a nice coat. Try it on.
   Monica: I don't like the color. Do they have a red or a blue coat?
3. **Monica:** Gloves? Why do I need gloves?
   Lydia: Try on these gloves. Believe me. You need gloves.
4. **Monica:** How do you like this coat?
   Lydia: It doesn't fit you. It's too big.
5. **Monica:** Do you like this sweater?
   Lydia: Yes, it looks good on you.

Unit 11

CD3·TR3
(Page 146)

Listen and show the time on the clocks.

a. What time is it? It's four o'clock.
b. What time is it? It's six thirty.
c. What time is it? It's eight fifteen.
d. What time is it? It's ten fifty-five.
e. What time is it? It's one twenty.
f. What time is it? It's ten forty-five.
g. What time is it? It's five ten.
h. What time is it? It's seven thirty.

CD3·TR6
(Page 150)

Listen to the conversation. Circle the correct answers about Pierre's day.

A: Where do you go to school, Pierre?
B: Bayside College.
A: How many days a week?
B: I go to school four days a week, Monday, Tuesday, Wednesday, and Thursday. I'm in an intensive program. School is in the morning, from 9:00 to 12:00.
A: Do you have a lot of homework?
B: Yes! About two hours a day. I eat lunch with my friends from school. And then, after lunch, I study with a friend. After that, I go to the library.
A: Do you work, too?
B: I don't work during the week. I work in a restaurant on Friday, Saturday, and Sunday.

CD3·TR7
(Page 150)

Listen to the conversation. Talk about Maria's day. Some of the sentences are negative.

A: Where do you go to school, Maria?
B: South Street Adult School.
A: How many days a week?
B: Two days a week. I go to school on Tuesday and Thursday night, from 7:00 to 9:00.
A: Do you have a lot of homework?
B: Yes! About an hour a night. But, I don't have time to study. I have two children, and I work. I'm busy all day. And at night, I'm tired.

CD3·TR8
(Page 152)

The Big Picture: Trouble with Math

Emily is sixteen years old and a sophomore in high school. Emily likes school, but she loves sports. She is busy from morning to night.

Emily has two alarm clocks. The first alarm clock rings at 6:00 a.m. Emily turns off the alarm clock, but she doesn't get up. The second alarm clock rings at 6:15. She gets up slowly. She gets dressed and eats breakfast. Then, she takes the bus to school. Emily goes to school from 7:30 to 2:00. She likes all her classes except math. Math is difficult for her.

At 2:00, Emily goes to the gym and puts on her uniform. Emily plays baseball. She is on the school baseball team. Every day after school she practices or she plays a game. Sometimes her mother or father comes to her games.

Emily gets home at 5:30 and takes a long shower. Then, her family eats dinner at 6:00. Emily does her homework from 7:00 to 8:00. Then, she talks on the phone, plays video games, or watches TV. Emily sets her alarm clocks and goes to bed at 11:00.

CD3·TR9
(Page 153) **Listen and write each sentence you hear.**

1. Emily goes to high school.
2. She feels tired in the morning.
3. She doesn't like math.
4. Emily doesn't play tennis.
5. She doesn't have a lot of homework.
6. She goes to bed at 11:00.

CD3·TR10
(Page 153) **E** **Listen to the conversation between Emily and her mother.** Complete the sentences.

Mom: Emily, your school grades are very good, except in math.

Emily: Mom, math is really hard.

Mom: Emily, you only study one hour a night. Then, you talk on the phone and watch TV. You need to spend more time on math.

Emily: Mom, I don't like math.

Mom: You usually do your homework from 7:00 to 8:00. You need to study one more hour. I want you to study math every night from 8:00 to 9:00. No TV, no computer, no cell phone from 7:00 to 9:00.

Emily: Mom!

Unit 12

CD3·TR12
(Page 160) **B** **Listen and complete.**

BREAKFAST: Hi, my name is Mike. In the morning, I am always in a hurry, so I eat a small breakfast at 7:15. I eat cereal and toast. I always have a cup of coffee. Then, I go to work.

LUNCH: Hi, my name is Jenny. I have lunch from 1:00 to 2:00. I like to have a large salad with Italian dressing. I have cucumbers, tomatoes, carrots, and chicken or shrimp on my salad. To drink, I like iced tea. Sometimes, I have a piece of fruit for dessert.

DINNER: Hi, my name is Sara. My parents, my brother, and I always have dinner together. We eat at 7:00. Our favorite dinner is chicken or pasta. I like to have cookies for dessert. Oh, and my brother and I drink milk or water.

CD3·TR13
(Page 163) **B** **Listen and complete.**

A: Hello?

B: Hi, honey. Guess who?

A: Hi, Mom! I'm so happy that you called.

B: Why Stacey? What's wrong?

A: Christopher is a fussy eater. He won't eat my food.

B: What? What do you mean?

A: Here's an example. I made spaghetti last night.

B: Good. All kids love spaghetti.

A: Well, I put vegetables in it; onions, broccoli, and spinach. He didn't eat it.

B: Why not?

A: He doesn't like vegetables.

B: All vegetables?

A: All vegetables.

B: How about pizza?

A: He doesn't like tomato sauce.

B: Okay, take off the tomato sauce.

A: He doesn't like cheese, either.

B: How about a hot dog?

A: He doesn't like hot dogs or hamburgers. Oh, and he doesn't like fruit.

B: What does he like?

A: He likes peanut butter, white bread, and milk.

B: Well, he's only six. You were a fussy eater, too. He will change.

A: I hope so. Thanks for listening, Mom.

B: You're very welcome, sweetheart.

CD3·TR14
(Page 167) **The Big Picture: At Mario's Italian Restaurant**

Faye: Hi, how are you this evening?

Emma: Hi, Faye! It's Friday, so here we are at your table again, right by the window.

Faye: It's nice to see you every Friday.

Troy: You're our favorite waitress.

Faye: Thank you. And, you're my favorite customers. What would you like to drink?

Emma: I'll have iced tea.

Troy: I'll have a soda.

Emma: Here are the menus. I'll be back with your drinks.

Troy: What are you going to have, Emma?

Emma: I think I'll have a green salad and the pasta. How about you?

Troy: I had pasta for lunch. I'll have a green salad and the chicken. Where's Faye?

Emma: Here she comes.

CD3·TR15
(Page 167) **Listen and look at the picture.** Then, read and circle.

Bob: How do you like the pizza, Ann?

Ann: It's good, but I always like the pizza here.

Lori: Me, too. I love cheese and pepperoni.

Matthew: Dad, could I have another soda?

Lori: Me, too.

Bob: Okay, I'll call the waitress.

Ann: Bob, this was a great idea. We're all tired on Friday nights. I like to go out for dinner on Fridays.

Bob: So do I.

Matthew: Me, too. Let's have pizza every Friday!

CD3·TR16
(Page 170) **Pronunciation: *I'll* Listen and write.**

1. I'll have a hamburger.
2. He'll have a steak.
3. She'll have a salad.
4. I'll have the pasta.
5. She'll have a soda.
6. He'll have ice cream.

Unit 13

CD3·TR17
(Page 176) **Listen and complete the questions.** Then, practice the conversation.

A: What do you do?

B: I'm a manicurist in a salon.

A: Do you like your job?

B: Yes, I do. I like it very much.

A: Do you work in the day or in the evening?

B: I work from 9:00 A.M. to 5:00 P.M.

A: Do you need English for your job?

B: Yes, I do. Many of the hotel guests speak English, and I like to talk to the guests.

A: Do you wear a uniform?

B: No, but I always wear an apron and gloves.

A: Do you receive benefits?

B: Yes, I do. I work full time, so I get health and dental care, sick days, and paid vacation.

A: That's great. Do you get tips?

B: Yes, I do. Sometimes I get big tips.

CD3·TR21
(Page 179) **Listen and answer the questions about Luis's job.**

I'm a valet at the hotel, so I park cars all day. I work part time, Tuesday to Sunday for four hours a night. When the hotel is busy, I park about sixty cars a night. I get a lot of tips. Maybe fifty people will give me a tip. Sometimes it's quiet, so I get a break.

CD3·TR22
(Page 179)

Listen and answer the questions about Jane's job.

I'm a housekeeper at the hotel. I start work at about 9:00 A.M. and I work until 5:30 P.M. There are more than 200 rooms in the hotel, and I am in charge of the third floor. My coworker and I work together, and we change thirty to forty beds a day. We clean thirty to forty rooms. We get fifteen to twenty tips per day.

CD3·TR23
(Page 182)

The Big Picture: The Sunrise Hotel

My name is Ricardo Lopez. This is the Sunrise Hotel, and I'm the evening manager. The Sunrise Hotel is a big hotel with more than 200 rooms. There's a restaurant, a bar, two swimming pools—one indoor and one outdoor, and tennis courts. Many tourists stay here when they visit.

The Sunrise has about 100 employees. We have desk clerks, housekeepers, bellhops, landscapers, and restaurant employees. We also have a van driver. He drives guests to the airport and to downtown for shopping. And, we have an electrician and a plumber who make repairs.

We need people for all three shifts. People who work at night make one dollar more an hour than day employees. Some employees work full time, but we also have many part-time positions.

We are always looking for employees. The salary is low, but the employees work hard. Many employees leave us when they find a job with a better salary. But, some people like the hours, and the workers like the tips. We have a friendly hotel here. Are you looking for a job? We have job openings now.

CD3·TR24
(Page 183)

Listen and write each question. Then, circle the answer.

1. What does Ricardo Lopez do?
2. Does the hotel have a pool?
3. Where does the van driver go?
4. Who makes repairs?
5. Do all the employees work full time?
6. How many employees does the hotel have?

CD3·TR25
(Page 183)

Listen. Who is the manager speaking to? Complete.

1. Please clean rooms 371 and 374.
2. Could you park the cars for these guests, please?
3. Table 4 needs more water and the dessert menu.
4. Do we have any empty rooms for Saturday?
5. Some of theses towels are not clean. What kind of detergent are you using?
6. The air conditioner in Room 424 isn't working. Please check it.
7. Three guests need to get to the airport.

Unit 14

CD3·TR32
(Page 191)

Listen and complete the sentences.

1. He has a toothache.
2. She has a backache.
3. I have a headache.
4. He has a stomachache.
5. I have an earache.

CD3·TR35
(Page 196)

The Big Picture: In the waiting room

Dr. Johnson's waiting room is very busy. It's early spring, and many patients are sick. Mrs. Jacob is Dr. Johnson's nurse. She's talking to Mrs. Jackson. She's a new patient, so she's going to fill out a patient information form. Mrs. Lee is reading a magazine. She has a bad cough. The doctor is going to listen to her chest. Mr. Green is 75 years old, and he's in good health. He's in the office for his checkup. He has a checkup once a year. Mrs. Rios and her daughter, Julia, are in the office, too. Julia's crying because she has a bad burn on her finger. She burned her finger on the stove. Mr. Patel is holding his head. His head hurts. He has a bad headache. Miss Gonzalez is sneezing and coughing. She has allergies, and she needs a prescription from Dr. Johnson. Mr. Henderson is talking to his son, Andy. Andy cut his arm and he needs a tetanus shot. He's nervous and scared because he doesn't like shots.

CD3·TR41
(Page 206) **Listen and write the sentences you hear.**

1. I'm not going to watch TV tonight.
2. She is not going to study this weekend.
3. We aren't going to take a test tomorrow.
4. They aren't going to rent a movie tonight.
5. He is going to go shopping on Saturday.
6. It isn't going to rain tomorrow.

CD3·TR43
(Page 207) **Listen and complete.**

1. I 'm going to vacuum my living room tomorrow.
2. The students are going to study after class.
3. Some students aren't going to do homework tonight.
4. My friend is going to visit this weekend.
5. My family and I are going to go to a wedding next month.
6. My brother isn't going to sleep late tomorrow morning.

CD3·TR44
(Page 210) **The Big Picture: A Trip to the Beach**

Al: We're going to leave in a few minutes. Come on! Get in the car, Emily.

Emily: But, Dad. My friend, Linda, is going to come with us, too.

Al: Okay, where is she?

Emily: Here she is!

Paula: Al! I'm going to go talk to the neighbors.

Al: Now? Paula, we're going to be late!

Paula: They're going to water the plants and walk the dog, Al.

Al: Oh, I forgot. Rico, what is that?

Rico: I'm going to go surfing, Dad. I'm going to take my surfboard.

Al: No, you're not. It's not going to fit in the car.

Rico: No problem, Dad. I'm going to put it on top.

Al: Hurry up, everybody. Come on, Pedro. Get in your car seat. Paula! Let's go!

Paula: Okay, I'm ready. Let's go.

Al: Great. Wait a minute. Where's my wallet?

Skills Index

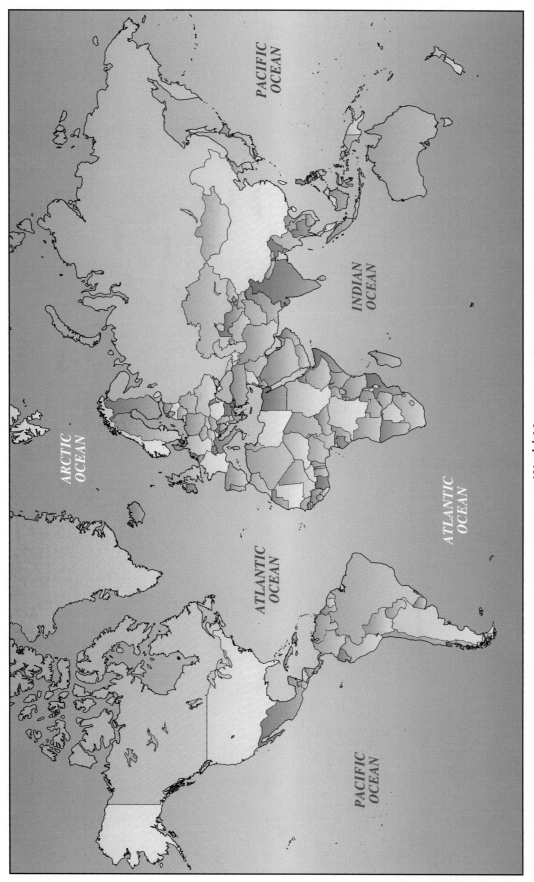

World Map

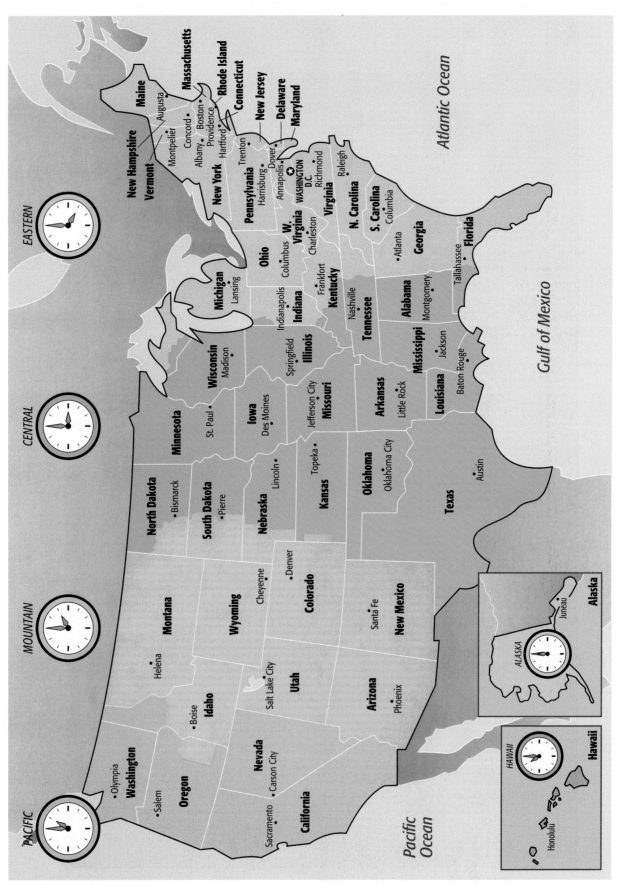

U.S. Map